Measure for Measure

Measure for Measure

Calorie and Carbohydrate controlled recipes compiled by
ELIZABETH O'REILLY
Dietitian to the British Diabetic Association

HEINEMANN HEALTH BOOKS
London

I should like to thank the following who helped
in the preparation of this book: Rona Begg,
S.R.D., who checked the recipes, Nick Evans of
the publishers, Ralph Dobson who drew the
illustrations, Tim McCarthy and Audrey Francis
of the British Diabetic Association, and
members of the Association who contributed
and tested recipes.

First published 1973
"Heinemann Health Books" are published by
William Heinemann Medical Books Ltd.
ISBN 0 433 24220 5

Printed by
The Whitefriars Press Ltd., London and Tonbridge, England

Contents

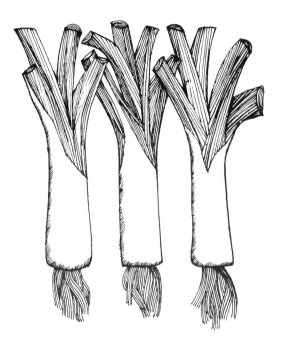

Conversion Tables

In calculating diabetic diets the Medical
Advisory Committee of the British Diabetic
Association agree that, for practical purposes
when converting Imperial to Metric weights,
one ounce should be regarded as equalling
30 grams (weight) although the precise figure is
28.4 grams.

WEIGHT

1 oz.	=	30 grams (g.)
2 oz.	=	60 grams (g.)
3 oz.	=	90 grams (g.)
4 oz. ($\frac{1}{4}$ lb.)	=	120 grams (g.)
8 oz. ($\frac{1}{2}$ lb.)	=	240 grams (g.)
12 oz. ($\frac{3}{4}$ lb.)	=	360 grams (g.)
16 oz. (1 lb.)	=	480 grams (g.)
2 lb. 2 oz. (approx.)	=	1 kilogram

LIQUID MEASURE

1 fl. oz.	=	25 millilitres (ml.)
2 fl. oz.	=	50 millilitres (ml.)
3 fl. oz.	=	75 millilitres (ml.)
4 fl. oz.	=	100 millilitres (ml.)
5 fl. oz. ($\frac{1}{4}$ pint)	=	125 millilitres (ml.)
10 fl. oz. ($\frac{1}{2}$ pint)	=	250 millilitres (ml.)
15 fl. oz. ($\frac{3}{4}$ pint)	=	375 millilitres (ml.)
20 fl. oz. (1 pint)	=	500 millilitres (ml.)
1000 millilitres	=	1 litre

OVEN TEMPERATURES

Electricity (°F)	Gas mark
250	$\frac{1}{4}$
275	$\frac{1}{2}$
300	1
325	2
350	3
375	4
400	5
425	6
450	7
475	8
500	9

Introduction

Most cooks know that good food is essential to healthy living but few have the nutritional knowledge to ensure balanced diets for themselves and their families. This book has been written to unravel the mystery surrounding dietary language and help them create wholesome meals.

Measure for Measure is a guide for successful eating. More than 350 recipes are set out in a dozen chapters covering soup to nuts. The carbohydrate-Calorie-Joule content for single servings are given at the beginning of each dish so that those watching weight can know how fattening the meal is before sitting down to the table. There is also a special section on culinary terms, a chapter on wines to take with meals, a list of nutritional values of all foods used in the book and a handy table for converting Metric to Imperial measures. The dishes in *Measure for Measure* have been selected with the greatest care and tested by an expert panel of cooks to give the best of home cooking. Ingredients are listed separately to make shopping easier.

Diabetics and non-diabetics alike will find this book useful. By following its recipes, diabetics will be able to introduce variety into their meals while still keeping to the diet prescribed by their doctor. Slimmers will be able to enjoy good food with a clear conscience as they will be able to gauge the Calorie or Joule content of each course. It should also simplify work in the kitchen: all recipes are suitable for the whole family so the cook need not prepare special dishes for the one member who has to follow a diet. Many of the recipes have been suggested by diabetics themselves and all the dishes make four servings except where otherwise stated.

To use *Measure for Measure* correctly, it is helpful to know a little about the constituents of food and the terms used by doctors and dietitians.

"Calories" or Joules are a measure of the energy and heat that your body can obtain from the food and drink that you consume. A rough guide to the number of Calories you can get from various types of food is:

> carbohydrates and protein: 4 Calories or approximately 17 Joules per Gram
>
> **fat**: 9 Calories or approximately 38 Joules per Gram

The number of Calories required by each individual depends on age, sex and occupation.

A person doing heavy manual work, or a sportsman taking a lot of exercise will require more Calories (3000-4000 a day) than someone leading a sedentary life (1500-2000 Calories a day). Ideally, your Calorie intake should equal your Calorie output.

One Calorie is the equivalent of 4.19 Joules so to convert your Calories into Joules multiply the number of Calories by 4.19.

Carbohydrates can be divided into two groups:

Starches: for example, flour, bread, potatoes and rice. They are likely to make up the greater part of your carbohydrate intake.

AND

Sugars: These are found in many foods but one type, sucrose, which occurs in white or brown sugar, cakes, jams, sweets, etc., is the most common sugar. The other types of sugars are lactose (found in milk) and fructose (in vegetables and fruits).

All starches and sugars are converted by your body into glucose and it is this sugar which pours into your bloodstream and gives you energy. If you consume more carbohydrates than your body uses up as energy, the excess will be turned into fat. So if you need to lose weight—cut down on the carbohydrates.

Proteins build and repair tissues as well as provide energy. Animals are the main source of these in the form of meat, fish, cheese, eggs and milk. Vegetables such as peas, beans and nuts are also sources of protein but they contain carbohydrate and/or fat as well. To get the right protein intake for good health you should include a mixture of both animal and vegetable protein foods in your diet.

Fats are a concentrated source of Calories. Butter and cream, dripping, suet and oils are almost pure fat. If you eat them in excess you will most certainly put weight on!

Vitamins. Anyone who has a well balanced and varied diet with plenty of fresh foods, particularly fruit and vegetables, need not fear that they are going short of vitamins.

Sweeteners

Sugar: You may be surprised to see sugar included in some of the recipes as many diet sheets specify "No sugar". This is done to prevent you from taking two or three teaspoons in tea or coffee which might add up to the total carbohydrate allowed for the meal. Sugar alone, added to drinks or sprinkled on breakfast cereal or fruit will raise the blood sugar quickly but combined in specific quantities with other ingredients in cooking, the effect is much slower, and recipes containing it can be worked into most diets.

Artificial sweeteners: One chapter is devoted to cooking with special sweeteners the main ones being sorbitol, fructose and saccharin and its derivatives. The recipes in this section are for two servings unless otherwise stated.

Sorbitol and fructose contain the same number of Calories or Joules as sugar and should not therefore be used if you want to lose weight. Incidentally, it is not considered advisable that more than 60 grams weight of fructose or Sorbitol should be taken during the day.

Saccharin can be used by diabetics and slimmers alike, but remember it should never be boiled as this produces a bitter taste.

To get the fullest advantage from this book, select menus that meet the nutritional needs of you and your family. Then sit down to meals that not only taste good but *are* good for you.

Calorie/Joule List

Each of the following contain **10 Grams Carbohydrate and 30 Calories (126 Joules)**

	Grams weight
Grapes, whole	60
Milk, sweetened condensed	20
Nectarines	90
Plantains	37
Sweet potato	37

Each of the following contain **10 Grams Carbohydrate and 40 Calories (168 Joules)**

	Grams weight
Apples, baked (with skin)	120
Apples, stewed	150
Apples, raw (with skin and core)	120
Apricots, dried, stewed	75
Apricots, fresh, stewed (with stones)	180
Bananas, ripe (without skin)	60
Bananas, green	60
Carrots, boiled	210
Cherries, raw (with stones)	120
Cherries, stewed (with stones)	120
Currants, dried	15
Damsons, stewed (with stones)	150
Dates (with stones)	20

	Grams weight
Dates (without stones)	15
Figs, dried, raw	20
Figs, dried, stewed	45
Gooseberries, dessert, raw	120
Greengages, raw (with stones)	90
Greengages, stewed (with stones)	120
Jelly, in packet	15
Melon (without skin)	210
Oranges (without peel)	120
Peaches, fresh (with stones)	120
Peaches, dried, raw	20
Peaches, raw (with skin and core)	120
Pears, stewed	150
Pineapple, fresh (edible part)	90
Plums, dessert, raw (with stones)	120
Potato crisps	20
Prunes, dry, raw (with stones)	30
Raisins, dried	15
Raspberries, raw	180
Raspberries, stewed	180
Rice, boiled	30
Strawberries, fresh, ripe	180
Sultanas, dried	15
Sweet corn (edible part)	45
Syrup	15
Tangerines (with peel)	180
Treacle	15

Each of the following contain 10 Grams Carbohydrate and 50 Calories (210 Joules)

	Grams weight
Allbran	20
Apricots, dried, raw	30
Apricots, fresh (with stones)	180
Beans, baked, tinned	60
Beans, butter, boiled	60
Beans, haricot, boiled	60
Beetroot, boiled	120
Bournvita	15
Bread, brown or white	20
Chestnuts	30
Corn on the cob (edible part)	90
Cornflakes or other unsweetened breakfast cereal	15
Cornflour, before cooking	15
Custard powder, before cooking	15
Figs, green, raw	120
Flour	15
Horlicks	15
Lentils, boiled	60
Macaroni, raw	15
Noodles, raw	15
Ovaltine	15
Parsnips, boiled	90
Peas, tinned	60
Plums, stewed (with stones)	240
Porridge, cooked with water	120
Potatoes, boiled	60
Potatoes, roast	45
Rice, before cooking	15
Ryvita	15
Sago, before cooking	15
Semolina, before cooking	15
Spaghetti, raw	15
Tapioca, before cooking	15

Each of the following contain 10 Grams Carbohydrate and 60 Calories (251 Joules)

	Grams weight
Beans, broad, boiled	150

	Grams weight
Biscuits, plain or semi-sweet	15
Lemon curd	22
Vitawheat	15

Each of the following contain 10 Grams Carbohydrate and 70 Calories (293 Joules)

	Millilitres
Milk, evaporated, unsweetened	75
Milk, powdered, skimmed (reconstituted according to directions)	175

	Grams weight
Potatoes, chipped	30
Potatoes, mashed	60

Each of the following contain 10 Grams Carbohydrate and the stated amount of Calories/Joules

	Grams weight	Calories	Joules
Almonds, shelled	240	1360	4441
Barcelona nuts, shelled	210	1323	4286
Brazil nuts, shelled	240	1464	4458
Chipolatas, cooked	90	246	1031
Cocoa powder	30	128	536
Ice cream, plain	60	112	469
Onions, fried	120	404	1693
Peanuts, shelled	120	684	2447
Sausages, cooked	90	279	1169
Walnuts, shelled	210	1092	4843
Yoghurt, plain	210	100	419

	Millilitres	Calories	Joules
Milk, fresh	175	133	557

	Pints	Milli-litres	Calories	Joules		Per 30 grams weight Calories	Joules
Ale, strong	$\frac{1}{2}$	250	147	616	Crab, boiled, shelled	36	151
Beer, bottled	1	500	160	670	Dover sole, steamed	24	100
Beer, draught					Dover sole, fried	68	285
bitter	$\frac{3}{4}$	375	135	566	Haddock, steamed	28	117
Cider, bottled,					Haddock, fried	50	210
dry	$\frac{3}{4}$	375	150	628	Haddock, smoked, steamed	28	117
Cider, bottled,					Hake, steamed	24	100
sweet	$\frac{1}{2}$	250	120	503	Halibut, steamed	37	155
Stout, bottled	$\frac{1}{2}$	250	100	419	Herrings, baked, in vinegar	50	210
					Kippers, baked	31	139
					Lemon sole, steamed	18	75
					Lemon sole, fried	62	260
					Lobster, boiled, shelled	34	142
					Oysters, raw	14	57

PROTEINS

	Per 30 grams weight Calories	Joules		Per 30 grams weight Calories	Joules
			Pilchards, canned fish only	54	226
Cheese			Plaice, steamed	26	109
Camembert	88	369	Plaice, fried	66	277
Cheddar	120	503	Prawns, shelled	30	126
Cheshire	110	461	Salmon, canned	84	352
Cream	232	972	Shrimps, shelled	32	134
Danish blue	103	427	Turbot, steamed	28	117
Edam	88	369	Whitebait, fried	152	637
Gorgonzola	112	469			
Gouda	96	402	**Meat**		
Gruyere	132	553	Bacon, fried	142	595
Parmesan	118	494	Beef, corned	66	277
Processed	106	444	Beef, silverside, boiled	86	360
Spread	82	344	Beef, roast	83	348
St. Ivel	108	452	Beef, steak, grilled	86	360
Stilton	135	566	Chicken, boiled (meat only)	58	243
Wensleydale	115	482	Chicken, roast (meat only)	54	226
			Ham, boiled (lean only)	62	260
			Liver, fried	74	310
Eggs			Luncheon meat, tinned	95	398
Boiled	46	193	Mutton, roast	83	348
Fried	68	285	Mutton chop, grilled		
Poached	45	189	(with bone)	108	452
			Pork, roast	90	377
Fish			Pork chop, grilled		
Cod, steamed	23	96	(with bone)	128	536
Cod, fried	40	168	Veal, roast	66	277

FATS

| | Per 30 grams weight | |
	Calories	Joules
Butter	226	947
Cream, single	62	260
Cream, double	131	549
Lard	262	1098
Margarine	226	947
Oils	264	1106
Suet	262	1098

Soups

Each recipe makes four servings except where otherwise stated

> Soak artichokes in cold water for at least half an hour, drain and scrub them thoroughly but do not peel.

Put in large saucepan with peeled onion and stock. Bring to boil and simmer for about 30 minutes or until artichokes and onion are very soft.

Rub through a sieve or purée in electric blender. If too thick, thin with water, add seasoning to taste and reheat.

Just before serving, add cream.

Artichoke Soup

Each serving 5 C. 105 Cals. (440 J.)

480 g. Jerusalem artichokes	150 ml. single
60 g. onions (1 small)	cream
600 ml. chicken stock	seasoning
(see recipe)	

Beetroot Soup

Each serving 10 C. 175 Cals. (733 J.)

360 g. beetroot	60 g. cabbage
120 g. onions (1 large)	120 g. cucumber
120 g. carrots	125 ml. sour cream
30 g. butter	seasoning
625 ml. brown stock (see recipe)	

> Peel carrots, beetroots and onions and chop finely. Cover with water, bring to the boil and simmer for 30 minutes. Drain and cool.

Rub vegetables through a sieve or purée in electric blender. Add butter, brown stock and cabbage.

Return to heat and simmer for a further 30 minutes. Just before serving season to taste and add sour cream and grated cucumber.

Serve hot.

Brown Stock*

Each serving Nil C. Negligible Cals. (Negligible J.)

480 g. shin of beef	60 g. onions (1 small)
480 g. beef bones	60 g. leeks
4 litres water	mixed herbs
60 g. carrots	seasoning

> Cut meat into small pieces. Trim or peel vegetables and chop.

Put meat, bones, vegetables and seasoning in large pan and add water.

Bring to boil and simmer for 3 to 4 hours. Leave to cool and skim fat from top. Strain to remove vegetables, meat and bones.

Store liquid in cool place as a basis for other soups, or serve reheated as a clear soup.

* As an alternative a beef bouillon cube may be used.

Cream of Carrot Soup

Each serving 20 C. 150 Cals. (628 J.)

480 g. carrots	125 ml. milk
60 g. turnips	50 ml. single cream
60 g. onions (1 small)	60 g. flour
30 g. lean bacon (trimmed)	1 teaspoon mixed
1 litre chicken stock	herbs
(see recipe)	seasoning

> Wash, peel and cut vegetables into small pieces and chop bacon finely. Put vegetables, bacon and herbs in large saucepan and add stock.

Bring to boil and simmer for $1\frac{1}{2}$ hours. Remove from heat. Mix flour with a little cold water to make a paste and add to the soup.

Rub through a sieve or purée in electric blender. Season to taste, add milk and return to pan.

Bring to boil and stir over low heat until it starts to thicken. Just before serving, stir in cream.

Cauliflower Soup

Each serving 10 C. 210 Cals. (880 J.)

480 g. cauliflower	1 litre chicken stock
(trimmed)	(see recipe)
30 g. flour	125 ml. single cream
30 g. butter	seasoning
1 egg yolk	

> Remove outer leaves from cauliflower, and break the rest into small pieces. Wash well.

Melt butter in pan and stir in flour to make a roux.

Add stock gradually stirring over low heat until it begins to thicken.

Add cauliflower, bring to boil and simmer until cauliflower is very tender.

Allow to cool, then rub through a sieve or purée in electric blender.

Season to taste.

Beat egg yolk and cream together and add to the purée.

Reheat before serving, but do not boil.

Mix flour with a little cold water to make a paste, and add it to the soup.

Rub through a sieve or purée in electric blender. Add milk.

Season to taste.

Return to pan, bring to boil and stir over low heat until the soup thickens.

Just before serving, add cream.

Cream of Chicken Soup

Negligible C. 100 Cals. (419 J.)

1 litre chicken stock (see recipe)	125 ml. single cream chopped parsley for
15 g. flour	garnishing
15 g. butter	seasoning

> Make a roux with butter and flour.

Add chicken stock gradually and stir until boiling.

Season to taste and simmer for 30 minutes.

Just before serving, add cream and sprinkle with parsley.

Cream of Celery Soup

Each serving 15 C. 170 Cals. (712 J.)

480 g. celery	60 g. flour
90 g. onions (1 medium)	125 ml. milk
1 litre chicken stock (see recipe)	50 ml. single cream seasoning

> Peel onions, wash and trim celery and dice.

Put vegetables and stock in saucepan, bring to boil and simmer for 1½ hours.

Remove from heat.

Chicken Stock*

Each serving Nil C. Negligible Cals. Negligible J.

1 chicken carcasse	4 litres water
120 g. onions (1 large)	mixed herbs
120 g. carrots	seasoning

> Put chicken carcasse, with peeled and chopped vegetables in large pan.
  Add seasoning, herbs and water.
  Bring to boil and simmer for 4 hours.
  Strain to remove bones and vegetables.
  Allow to cool then skim off fat.
  Store in cool place.
  Serve chilled or reheated, or use as base for other soups.

* *As an alternative to this recipe a chicken bouillon cube may be used.*

Fish Stock

Nil C. Negligible Cals. (Negligible J.)

480 g. fish trimmings	mixed herbs
60 g. onion (1 small)	seasoning
2 bay leaves	3 litres water

> Peel onion.
  Put all ingredients in large pan, bring to boil and simmer for 2 hours.
  Strain and use as required.

Cream of Lettuce Soup

Each serving 5 C. 155 Cals. (649 J.)

480 g. lettuce (outer leaves can be used)	15 g. butter
	250 ml. milk
500 ml. chicken stock (see recipe)	50 ml. double cream
30 g. onion ($\frac{1}{2}$ small)	seasoning

> Wash and shred lettuce. Peel and chop onion.

Melt butter in pan and cook onion until transparent.
  Add lettuce, stock and seasoning to the onion.
  Cover, bring to boil and simmer for 15 minutes.
  Rub through sieve or purée in electric blender.
  Add milk and seasoning.
  Reheat but do not boil and just before serving, add cream.

Consommé

Each serving Nil C. Negligible Cals. (Negligible J.)

1 marrow bone	120 g. onions (1 large)
240 g. shin of beef (trimmed)	1$\frac{1}{2}$ litres water
	seasoning

> Peel and chop onion, and cut meat into pieces.
  Put, with other ingredients, in large saucepan.
  Bring to boil and simmer for 1$\frac{1}{2}$ hours.
  Remove bone.
  Strain through fine sieve.
  Return to pan and bring to boil if serving hot.
  Chill in refrigerator if serving cold.

Mulligatawny Soup

Each serving 10 C. 505 Cals. (2112 J.)

480 g. scragend mutton	60 g. cooking apples

15 g. bacon (trimmed)	30 g. lard
60 g. onions (1 small)	1½ litres water
60 g. carrots	juice of 1 lemon
60 g. turnips	mixed herbs
15 g. flour	seasoning
15 g. curry powder	

> Simmer mutton in water for 1 hour, then skim off surplus fat.

Peel and dice the vegetables and apple. Dice bacon.

Melt fat in another pan, fry onions and bacon, then add flour and curry powder blending in with a little stock.

Add onion and bacon mixture, remaining vegetables, apple, herbs, seasoning and lemon juice to meat and stock.

Bring to boil and simmer for 1 to 1½ hours.

Remove meat and bacon and set aside.

Rub vegetables through a sieve or reduce to purée in an electric blender.

Dice meat and bacon and add to purée.

Return to heat and bring to boil before serving.

Cream of Mushroom Soup

Each serving 5 C. 180 Cals. (754 J.)

480 g. mushrooms	15 g. cornflour
250 ml. milk	seasoning
50 ml. vegetable oil	

> Wash mushrooms and peel if skin is leathery. If button variety, leave skin on. Do not remove stalks. Chop roughly.

Heat oil in saucepan, add mushrooms and cook gently until tender.

Add a quarter of the milk and rub through sieve, or purée in electric blender.

Mix cornflour to a paste with a little of the cold milk, add remaining milk, bring to boil and stir over low heat until it thickens.

Add mushroom purée and seasoning to taste.

Return to heat and simmer for 5 minutes before serving.

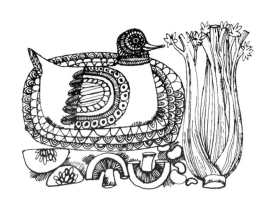

French Onion Soup

Each serving 5 C. 150 Cals. (628 J.)

480 g. onions (4 large)	1 litre chicken stock
30 g. butter	(see recipe)
25 ml. vegetable oil	seasoning

> Peel and slice onions thinly.

Melt butter and oil together in saucepan over low heat.

Add onions and cook, without lid, stirring from time to time until onions are golden brown.

Add stock, bring to boil and simmer over low heat for 40 to 45 minutes.

Add seasoning to taste and serve hot.

Smoked Haddock Soup

Each serving 5 C. 235 Cals. (985 J.)

480 g. smoked haddock	125 ml. single cream
30 g. butter	squeeze lemon juice
60 g. onions (1 small)	1 litre water
30 g. carrots	seasoning
30 g. flour	

> Wash fish, remove skin and bones and cut into small pieces.

Peel and dice vegetables.

Melt butter in large pan, add vegetables and sauté until onion is transparent.

Add flour and stir until well blended.

Add fish and water and stir until boiling.

Simmer for 1 hour.

Rub through a sieve or purée in electric blender.

Season to taste, return to pan and reheat.

Just before serving, add lemon juice and cream.

Cream of Spinach Soup

Each serving 5 C. 180 Cals. (754 J.)

720 g. prepared spinach	250 ml. milk
30 g. onions ($\frac{1}{2}$ small)	50 ml. double cream
15 g. butter	grated nutmeg
50 ml. chicken stock	seasoning
(see recipe)	

> Make sure spinach is really clean, then put it in a saucepan with just enough salted boiling water to prevent it sticking.

Boil for 3 minutes turning spinach over after about a minute to ensure it is cooked evenly.

Drain and press between two plates to remove as much water as possible.

Melt butter in the pan and cook the peeled and chopped onion until transparent.

Add stock, spinach and cover.

Bring to boil and simmer gently for 20 minutes.

Rub through sieve or purée in electric blender.

Return to pan, add milk, a little nutmeg and seasoning to taste.

Reheat but do not boil.

Just before serving, add the cream.

Tomato Soup

Each serving 15 C. 90 Cals. (377 J.)

720 g. fresh tomatoes	$1\frac{1}{4}$ litres water
60 g. onions (1 small)	mixed herbs
125 ml. single cream	seasoning

> Peel tomatoes and chop roughly.

Peel and dice onion very finely.

Put tomatoes, onions, herbs and seasoning in pan with water.

Bring to boil and simmer for $1\frac{1}{2}$ hours.

Rub through a sieve or purée in an electric blender.

Return to pan and reheat.

Just before serving, add cream.

Mixed Vegetable Soup I

Each serving 10 C. 35 Cals. (160 J.)

480 g. turnip	2 litres water
240 g. swede	mixed herbs
60 g. celery	seasoning
60 g. carrots	

> Peel and dice all vegetables, and put them with water, herbs and seasoning in a saucepan.
 Bring to boil and simmer for 1½ hours.
 Rub through a sieve or purée in an electric blender.
 Return to pan and reheat before serving.

Mixed Vegetable Soup II

Each serving 10 C. 40 Cals. (168 J.)

240 g. onions (2 large)	2 litres water
240 g. carrots	mixed herbs
240 g. tomatoes	seasoning

> Wash and peel vegetables, and dice finely.
 Place in large saucepan with water, herbs and seasoning.
 Bring to boil and simmer for 1½ hours.
 Rub through a sieve or purée in electric blender.
 Reheat and serve.

Vichyssoise

Each serving 20 C. 230 Cals. (964 J.)

300 g. leeks (trimmed)	chopped parsley or
300 g. peeled potatoes	fresh chives

1 litre chicken stock	seasoning
(see recipe)	
125 ml. double cream	

> Wash leeks well and slice finely.
 Dice potatoes and put in pan with leeks and stock.
 Bring to boil and simmer, in covered pan, for 1 hour.
 Rub through sieve or purée in electric blender.
 Season to taste.
 Return to pan and reheat but do not boil.
 Just before serving, add cream and garnish with parsley or chives.

Watercress Soup

Each serving 5 C. 115 Cals. (482 J.)

1 large bunch watercress	100 ml. single cream
15 g. butter	1 litre chicken stock
60 g. onion (1 small)	(see recipe)
120 g. potato (peeled)	seasoning

> Wash watercress thoroughly and remove coarse stalks. Set aside a few sprigs for garnishing.
 Melt butter in saucepan and fry peeled and sliced onion until transparent.
 Add stock, watercress and diced potatoes.
 Bring to boil and simmer for 30 minutes.
 Rub through sieve or purée in electric blender.
 Season to taste.
 Reheat and, just before serving, add cream and garnish with watercress sprigs.

Egg and Cheese

Each recipe makes four servings except where otherwise stated

Bacon and Egg Flan

Each serving 15 C. 390 Cals. (1634 J.)

90 g. shortcrust pastry   a few slices of tomato
  (or 120 g. made pastry) chopped parsley
  using 90 g. flour   mixed herbs
120 g. bacon rashers   seasoning
5 eggs

> Make pastry and roll out to line 8-inch flan tin.
    Trim bacon and lay rashers on base of flan.
    Beat eggs, add parsley, herbs and seasoning and pour over the bacon.
    Top with tomato slices.
    Bake at 425° F (Mark 6) for 30 to 40 minutes.

Cheese and Bacon Snack

Each serving 15 C. 315 Cals. (1320 J.)

4 slices bread   120 g. onion (1 large)
  (120 g.)   120 g. streaky bacon
120 g. grated Cheddar   rashers (chopped)
  cheese

> Chop onion very finely.
    Toast bread on one side.
    On untoasted side of each slice place a quarter of the onion, cheese and bacon.
    Put under hot grill until cheese is melted and bacon crisp.

Cheese and Chicken Pancakes

Each pancake 5 C. 200 Cals. (838 J.)

120 g. cooked chicken   chopped parsley
60 g. onion (1 small)   oil for frying
2 eggs   100 ml. water
60 g. flour   seasoning
60 g. grated Cheddar cheese

> Mince chicken and onion and mix with parsley.

Melt butter in pan, add chicken mixture and fry until onion is transparent.

Add seasoning.

Make batter by mixing eggs, flour and water and season to taste. Leave to stand for an hour.

Heat oil in omelette pan and make 8 pancakes cooked on one side only.

As cooked remove from pan and place on greased paper with cooked side up.

Spread each pancake with chicken mixture and roll.

Place on greased pan, sprinkle with grated cheese and brown under hot grill.

Cheese and Chive Omelette Soufflé

Each serving Nil C. 255 Cals. (1068 J.)

240 g. cottage cheese	pinch of dry
6 eggs	mustard
30 g. butter	seasoning
1 dessertspoon chopped chives	

> Separate egg and mix yolks with cheese, chives, mustard and seasoning

Whisk whites until stiff and fold with metal spoon into mixture.

Melt butter in frying pan, divide mixture into four to make individual omelettes.

When risen and set, brown under grill.

Cheese Croquettes

Each croquette 10 C. 255 Cals. (1068 J.)

1 whole egg	250 ml. milk
2 egg yolks	45 g. dry breadcrumbs
100 g. grated Cheddar cheese	vegetable oil for frying
50 g. butter or margarine	pinch of cayenne pepper
50 g. plain flour	seasoning

> Make a roux with butter and flour.

Add milk gradually, bring to boil and stir over low heat until sauce thickens.

Add cayenne pepper and remove from heat.

Add cheese and beaten egg yolks to mixture and season.

Chill in refrigetator.

Divide into 8 croquettes, and return to refrigerator until ready to use.

Beat whole egg, dip croquettes in egg and roll in breadcrumbs.

Deep fry in smoking oil and serve hot.

Cheese Eggs

Each serving Nil C. 305 Cals. (1278 J.)

4 eggs	50 ml. single
120 g. grated Cheddar cheese	cream
30 g. butter or margarine	seasoning

> Butter 1 large or 4 individual ovenproof dishes and sprinkle with half the cheese.

Break eggs gently over the cheese, pour on cream and season.

Sprinkle with remaining cheese.

Bake at 400° F (Mark 5) for 10 minutes.

Cheese Loaf

16 slices. Each 10 C. 130 Cals. (545 J.)

240 g. self-raising flour	90 g. margarine
1 egg	1 level teaspoon
90 g. grated Cheddar cheese	dry mustard
125 ml. milk	seasoning

> Sieve flour, add cheese, mustard and seasoning and rub in margarine to consistency of breadcrumbs.

Add beaten egg and milk to bind mixture.

Put in greased bread tin and bake at 375° F (Mark 4) for 45 minutes.

Turn out, leave to cool and cut into 16 slices.

Cheese Pudding

Each serving 20 C. 390 Cals. (1634 J.)

700 ml. milk	4 eggs
80 g. soft breadcrumbs	1 level teaspoon made
120 g. grated Cheddar	mustard
cheese	seasoning

> Heat milk and pour over breadcrumbs.

Separate eggs, beat yolks and add with the grated cheese to milk and breadcrumbs.

Add mustard and seasoning and mix well.

Beat egg whites until stiff and fold into mixture.

Pour into greased oven-proof dish and bake at 375° F (Mark 4) until risen and slightly brown. (Approximately 30 minutes.)

Cheese Savoury

Each serving Negligible C. 360 Cals. (1508 J.)

240 g. tomatoes	125 ml. double cream
3 eggs	1 teaspoon dry
120 g. grated Cheddar	mustard
cheese	seasoning

> Slice tomatoes and place on base of lightly greased oven-proof dish reserving a few slices for decoration.

Separate eggs, mix yolks with grated cheese, cream, dry mustard and seasoning.

Whisk egg whites until stiff and fold into mixture.

Pour over tomatoes and decorate with reserved slices.

Bake at 400° F (Mark 5) for 20 minutes.

Cheese Scramble

Each serving Negligible C. 270 Cals. (1131 J.)

6 eggs	60 g. grated Cheddar
100 ml. milk	cheese
30 g. butter or margarine	seasoning

> Beat eggs and milk together, add grated cheese and season.

Melt butter in large pan.

Add egg mixture and cook over low heat stirring all the time until it thickens.

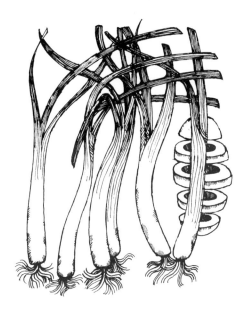

Cheese Soufflé

Each serving 10 C. 375 Cals. (1571 J.)

3 egg yolks	120 g. grated Cheddar cheese
4 egg whites	250 ml. milk
45 g. flour	¼ teaspoon mustard powder
45 g. butter or margarine	seasoning

> Grease medium-sized soufflé dish and tie foil or grease-proof paper on outside to at least 2 inches above rim.

Make a roux with butter and flour, add milk gradually, bring to boil and stir over low heat until sauce thickens.

Stir in cheese and leave to cool.

Separate eggs, beat yolks well and add to sauce.

Beat whites until stiff and fold into mixture. Season to taste.

Bake for 40 minutes at 400° F (Mark 5).

Remove foil or paper and serve immediately.

Cheese Straws

20 straws. Each 5 C. 50 Cals. (210 J.)

90 g. self-raising flour	pinch of cayenne pepper
45 g. butter or margarine	
60 g. grated Cheddar cheese	½ teaspoon mustard powder
1 egg yolk	

> Mix flour, cheese, mustard and cayenne pepper together and rub in butter to consistency of breadcrumbs.

Mix to stiff dough with egg yolk. (If necessary, add a little water to get right consistency.)

Roll out thinly and cut into 20 straws.

Lightly dust a baking tin with flour and bake straws at 350° F (Mark 3) for 10 to 15 minutes.

Cottage Eggs

Each serving Nil C. 335 Cals. (1403 J.)

11

8 hard boiled eggs	chopped parsley
120 g. cottage cheese	seasoning
with chives	lettuce
100 ml. double cream	
1 teaspoon made mustard	

> Shell and cut egg in half lengthwise.

Remove yolks and mash with cheese, cream, mustard and seasoning.

Fill egg whites with the mixture, sprinkle with chopped parsley and serve on bed of lettuce.

Curried Eggs (Cold)

Each serving Negligible C. 380 Cals. (1592 J.)

4 hard boiled eggs	50 g. double cream
100 ml. mayonnaise	juice of $\frac{1}{2}$ lemon
(see recipe)	salt
15 g. curry powder	boiling water
5 g. castor sugar	mustard and cress

> Mix curry powder and sugar with enough boiling water to make a smooth paste. Stir in lemon juice.

Mix paste and mayonnaise together and stir in cream to make a soft coating sauce. Add salt to taste.

Shell eggs and cut in half lengthwise, lay in dish, coat with sauce and garnish with mustard and cress.

Curried Eggs (Hot)

Each serving 10 C. 240 Cals. (1006 J.)

8 hard boiled eggs	250 ml. chicken
15 g. butter or margarine	stock
120 g. onion (1 large)	(see recipe)
120 g. prepared apple	juice of $\frac{1}{2}$ lemon
15 g. curry powder	salt
15 g. flour	

> Peel and chop onion and apple finely and fry, in the melted butter, over low heat until golden brown.

Blend in flour, curry powder, salt and lemon juice.

Add stock, bring to boil and stir over low heat until mixture thickens.

Pour over shelled eggs and serve hot.

Devilled Eggs

Each serving Nil C. 230 Cals. (964 J.)

4 hard boiled eggs	chopped parsley
60 g. anchovy fillets	cayenne pepper
45 g. butter or margarine	lettuce

> Cut eggs in half lengthwise, and remove yolks.

Chop finely or mince anchovy fillets and blend with yolks, butter, cayenne pepper and parsley.

Fill whites with mixture and serve on bed of lettuce.

Eggs Florentine

Each serving Negligible C. 290 Cals. (1215 J.)

360 g. prepared fresh or frozen spinach
4 eggs

90 g. grated Cheddar cheese	150 ml. single cream seasoning

> Cook spinach, drain well and chop finely.

Put spinach on base of shallow lightly-greased oven-proof dish.

Break eggs carefully on to the spinach spacing them out to cover top as evenly as possible.

Pour on cream, season and sprinkle with grated cheese.

Bake at 350° F (Mark 3) for 25 minutes.

Egg and Liver Sausage Cocottes

Each serving Negligible C. 275 Cals. (1152 J.)

120 g. liver sausage	paprika
4 eggs	salt
100 ml. double cream	

> Skin sausage and cut into four slices.

Using individual oven-proof dishes, place a slice of sausage in each.

Break an egg carefully into each dish and add salt to taste.

Pour a quarter of the cream over each egg and sprinkle with paprika.

Bake at 350° F (Mark 3) for 10 minutes.

Egg and Tomato Slice

4 slices. Each 10 C. 360 Cals. (1508 J.)

4 eggs	180 g. tomato
120 g. bacon rashers	375 ml. milk

60 g. grated Cheddar cheese	125 ml. water
120 g. onion (1 large)	½ teaspoon mixed herbs seasoning

> Skin and cut tomatoes into slices.

Remove rind and chop bacon, peel and chop onion. Fry together lightly in the bacon fat.

Add tomatoes and herbs, cook for a further minute.

Place in greased oven-proof dish.

Beat egg and add milk and water, season and pour over tomato mixture.

Sprinkle with grated cheese and bake at 350° F (Mark 3) for 45 minutes.

Serve hot.

Eggs in Onion Sauce

Each serving 10 C. 410 Cals. (1718 J.)

4 hard boiled eggs	50 ml. cooking oil
45 g. margarine	
45 g. flour	120 g. onion (1 large)
60 g. grated Cheddar cheese	
500 ml. chicken stock (see recipe)	mixed herbs seasoning

> Chop onion, cook in heated oil in large pan until transparent and set aside.

Make a roux with margarine and flour, add stock gradually, bring to boil and stir over heat until the sauce thickens.

Add onions, herbs and seasoning.

Cover pan and simmer gently for 10 minutes stirring from time to time.

Cut eggs in half lengthwise and place them in lightly greased oven-proof dish.

Over

Pour on sauce, sprinkle with grated cheese and brown under hot grill.

Macaroni Cheese

Each serving 25 C. 360 Cals. (1508 J.)

115 g. macaroni (raw)	250 ml. water
30 g. flour	120 g. grated
30 g. butter or margarine	Cheddar cheese
250 ml. milk	seasoning

> Make a roux with butter and flour.

Add milk and water gradually, bring to boil and stir over low heat until sauce thickens.

Add seasoning.

Grease oven-proof dish and put alternate layers of macaroni and cheese ending with cheese.

Pour on sauce and bake for 20 minutes at 350° F (Mark 3).

Onion and Mushroom Omelette

Each serving Nil C. 305 Cals. (1278 J.)

8 eggs	50 ml. cooking oil
60 g. onion (1 small)	seasoning
60 g. mushrooms	

> Peel and chop onion and mushrooms.

Heat most of the oil in a pan reserving enough to cook omelettes.

Fry together mushrooms and onion until latter is transparent.

Set aside and keep hot.

Beat eggs well and season.

Heat remaining oil in omelette pan.

Divide egg mixture into four and make individual omelettes, filling each with the onion and mushroom mixture before folding.

Serve hot.

Salmon Soufflé

Each serving 10 C. 350 Cals. (1467 J.)

120 g. canned salmon	60 g. grated
30 g. butter or	Cheddar cheese
margarine	50 ml. single cream
30 g. flour	250 ml. milk
4 eggs	seasoning

> Grease medium sized soufflé dish, and tie foil or greaseproof paper outside to at least 2 inches above rim.

Make a roux with butter and flour, add milk gradually, bring to boil and stir over low heat until sauce thickens.

Add cheese and cook until this melts.

Allow to cool.

Separate eggs, beat yolks with cream and add to sauce.

Flake and add salmon and season.

Beat egg whites until stiff and fold into mixture.

Pour in the soufflé dish and bake at 350° F (Mark 3) for 40 minutes.

Spanish Soufflé

Each serving Nil C. 155 Cals. (649 J.)

4 eggs   seasoning
100 ml. single cream

> Separate eggs, beat yolks and stir in cream. Whisk whites until stiff and fold into the yolks and cream.
   Season and pour into buttered soufflé dish. Bake at 325° F (Mark 2) for 25 minutes.

Spinach Roulade

Each serving 10 C. 305 Cals. (1278 J.)

4 eggs	180 g. mushrooms
240 g. prepared	30 g. flour
fresh or frozen	125 ml. milk
spinach	100 ml. double cream
30 g. grated	seasoning
Cheddar cheese	

> Line swiss roll tin with oiled greaseproof paper.
   Cook spinach, drain, cool and rub through sieve or purée in electric blender.
   Separate eggs and add beaten yolks, half the butter and the cheese and mix into the purée.
   Whisk egg whites until stiff and fold into the mixture.
   Pour into the tin and bake at 375° F (Mark 4) for 10 minutes.
   Wash and dice mushrooms and fry in remaining butter.
   Blend in flour, add milk gradually and stir over low heat until the sauce thickens.
   Season, remove from heat and add cream.
   Turn out spinach, spread with mushroom mixture and roll up like a swiss roll.
   Serve hot.

Spinach Soufflé

Each serving 10 C. 330 Cals. (1388 J.)

3 egg yolks	45 g. butter or margarine
4 egg whites	30 g. grated Cheddar
480 g. prepared	cheese
fresh or frozen	250 ml. milk
spinach	25 ml. single cream
45 g. flour	seasoning

> Grease medium-sized soufflé dish and tie foil or greaseproof paper on outside to at least 2 inches above rim.
   If spinach is fresh, wash well and cook without added water.
   Follow instructions on packet for cooking frozen spinach.
   Drain well, add cream and rub through sieve or purée in electric blender.
   Make a roux with butter and flour, add milk gradually, bring to boil and stir over low heat until sauce thickens.
   Add spinach and cheese, mix well and allow to cool. Stir in egg yolks.
   Beat egg whites until stiff and fold into mixture.
   Season to taste.
   Bake for 40 minutes at 400° F (Mark 5).
   Remove foil or paper and serve immediately.

Tomato with Egg Stuffing

Each serving Negligible C. 155 Cals. (640 J.)

8 medium-sized	30 g. butter or margarine
tomatoes (240 g.)	chopped parsley
4 eggs	seasoning

> Cut tops off tomatoes, scoop out flesh and place tomato cases in buttered oven-proof dish.

Beat eggs, add tomato flesh, season and pour into the cases.

Bake at 325° F (Mark 2) for 10 to 15 minutes.

Serve hot garnished with chopped parsley.

Tomato Scramble

Each serving Negligible C. 320 Cals. (1341 J.)

8 eggs	50 ml. cooking oil
120 g. tomato	seasoning
100 ml. milk	

> Skin and dice tomatoes and cook gently in heated oil.

Beat eggs with milk and season.

Pour eggs and milk over tomatoes and stir over low heat until mixture thickens.

Welsh Rarebit

Each serving 15 C. 370 Cals. (1550 J.)

4 slices bread each 30 g.	1 egg
240 g. grated Cheddar cheese	1 teaspoon Worcester sauce
50 ml. ale	$\frac{1}{4}$ teaspoon mustard powder
15 g. butter or margarine	seasoning

> Toast bread on one side.

Melt butter in pan, add cheese and stir over low heat until melted. Remove from heat.

Beat egg with ale, Worcester sauce, seasoning and mustard powder and stir into butter and cheese mixture.

Divide evenly and spoon on to the uncooked side of the toast.

Brown under hot grill.

Cheese Pie

Each serving 20 C. 280 Cals. (1172 J.)

480 g. potatoes	120 g. tomato
2 hard boiled eggs	30 g. butter
90 g. grated cheese	seasoning
1 medium onion (120 g.)	

> Peel potatoes, slice and cook in boiling water until soft. Then mash.

Remove shells from eggs, chop finely and add, with 60 g. grated cheese, to the hot mashed potatoes.

Chop onion and fry in butter until transparent. Add sliced tomato and cook for a few minutes.

Grease an oven-proof dish and spread half potato mixture in the bottom. Put onion and tomato on this base and cover with remaining potato.

Sprinkle with remaining 30 g. cheese and bake at 425° F (mark 6) for 40 minutes.

Fish

Each recipe makes four servings except where otherwise stated

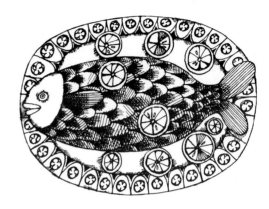

Casserole Sicilian

Each serving 10 C. 170 Cals. (712 J.)

500 g. cod or other
   white fish fillets
240 g. fresh or
   frozen runner beans
300 g. tinned tomato soup
   (undiluted)

1 teaspoon
   Worcester sauce
seasoning

> Cook beans, drain and put in oven-proof dish.
   Wash fish, remove any skin and bones and cut into 1-inch pieces.
   Add to beans.
   Heat but do not boil soup, pour over fish mixture. Add Worcester sauce and seasoning.
   Bake at 300° F (Mark 1) for 35 minutes in covered dish.

Cod with Bacon

Each serving Nil C. 360 Cals. (1508 J.)

720 g. cod fillets
240 g. lean bacon rashers

chopped parsley
seasoning

> Skin and bone fish. Cut into four portions. Trim bacon and wrap a rasher round each piece of cod.
   Season and place in oven-proof dish.
   Bake at 375° F (Mark 4) for 25 minutes.
   Garnish with parsley before serving.

Cod with Cheese

Each serving Nil C. 380 Cals. (1592 J.)

960 g. cod
60 g. grated Cheddar
   cheese

60 g. butter or
   margarine
seasoning

> Remove skin and bones from fish and cut into four.

Melt butter and brush grill pan and each piece of fish with butter. Season to taste.

Grill fish for 5 minutes on each side, sprinkle with cheese and grill for a further 2 minutes.

Cod Creole

Each serving 5 C. 340 Cals. (1425 J.)

1 kg. cod fillets	60 g. green peppers
120 g. onion (1 large)	50 ml. cooking oil
240 g. tomatoes	200 ml. water
180 g. mushrooms	seasoning

> Peel and chop finely onions, tomatoes, and mushrooms.

De-seed and chop peppers

Remove skin and any bones from fish, and cut into four. Poach gently for 15 minutes in the water

Drain, reserving the liquid, and keep fish hot.

Melt oil in pan and cook onion until transparent. Add peppers, tomatoes, mushrooms and seasoning. Cook for a few minutes.

Add reserved liquid and simmer until vegetables are very soft.

Add fish and reheat but do not boil, before serving.

Devilled Cod

Each serving Negligible C. 280 Cals. (1173 J.)

1 kg. cod fillet	30 g. tomato chutney
30 g. margarine	1 level teaspoon dry
1 level teaspoon curry	mustard
powder	seasoning

> Remove skin and bones from fish and cut into four.

Place under grill and cook one side only.

Remove from heat and turn over.

Cream margarine and beat in curry powder, mustard, chutney and seasoning. Spread mixture on uncooked side of fish and return to grill until the cod is cooked.

Coley Duglère

Each serving 10 C. 425 Cals. (1634 J.)

1 kg. coley	30 g. flour
300 g. tomatoes	1 small onion (60 g.)
125 ml. dry red wine	250 ml. milk
60 g. butter	seasoning

> Remove skin and bones from fish and cut into four pieces.

Put in oven-proof dish.

Peel and dice onions and tomatoes and sprinkle over fish.

Pour on wine and dot with half the butter.

Bake at 400° F (Mark 5) for 30 minutes.

Meanwhile make a roux with flour and remaining butter, add milk gradually, bring to boil and stir over low heat until sauce thickens.

Season and pour over the fish and vegetables.

Return to oven and bake for a further 10 minutes.

Coley Fricasse

Each serving 10 C. 220 Cals. (922 J.)

480 g. coley fillets	30 g. butter or
60 g. carrots	margarine
60 g. onion (1 small)	30 g. flour
60 g. tomatoes	125 ml. milk
60 g. fresh or frozen	375 ml. water
peas	seasoning

> Peel and dice finely carrots, onion and tomatoes.

Remove skin and any bones from fish and cook gently in water for 10 to 15 minutes. Drain, reserving the liquid, and keep coley warm in oven-proof dish in cool oven.

Simmer carrots, onions, tomatoes and peas in the fish liquid for 15 minutes. When vegetables are cooked, remove from the liquid and spread them over the fish. Return to oven.

Make a roux with butter and flour, gradually add the liquid in which fish and vegetables have been cooked, bring to boil and stir over low heat until the sauce thickens.

Add milk to the sauce, return to boil and stir over heat for a few more minutes.

Season to taste and pour sauce over the fish and vegetables.

Fish Cakes

8 cakes. Each 5 C. 85 Cals. (356 J.)

240 g. cooked cod or other white fish

240 g. mashed potatoes	1 egg
30 g. butter or	mixed herbs
margarine	seasoning

> Remove skin and bones and flake fish. Blend with mashed potatoes.

Melt butter and mix well with the fish and potatoes

Beat in egg, mixed herbs and seasoning.

Form into 8 cakes and cook under grill for 3 to 4 minutes on each side.

Fish Casserole

Each serving Negligible C. 245 Cals. (1027 J.)

960 g. cod or other	30 g. onion
white fish	($\frac{1}{2}$ small)
100 ml. sour cream	mixed herbs
30 g. tomatoes	seasoning

> Remove skin and bones from fish, cut into small pieces and put in oven-proof dish.

Peel and chop onions and tomatoes and sprinkle over the fish.

Pour on sour cream, add herbs and seasoning, and bake in covered dish at 350° F (Mark 3) for 45 minutes.

Fish and Cheese Pie

Each serving 5 C. 220 Cals. (922 J.)

720 g. cod or other	120 g. tomatoes
white fish	1 egg
30 g. grated Cheddar	125 ml. milk
cheese	chopped parsley
60 g. onion (1 small)	seasoning

> Remove skin and bones from fish and cut into small pieces.

Peel and chop onion and peel and slice tomatoes.

Put fish in oven-proof dish with onion, parsley, cheese and seasoning.

Beat egg and milk together and pour over fish mixture.

Top with tomato slices and bake at 350° F (Mark 3) for 1 hour.

Fish Fried in Batter

Each serving 10 C. 430 Cals. (1802 J.)

1 kg. cod or other white fish	125 ml. milk oil for frying
45 g. flour	water to mix
2 eggs	seasoning

> Remove skin and bones from fish and cut into four.

Put flour in bowl, break in eggs and mix together.

Add milk gradually, season and beat in water until a thick coating consistency is reached

Coat each piece of fish with the batter making sure that all the batter is used.

Heat oil and, when smoking, fry the fish until golden brown.

Fish Pie

Each serving 25 C. 415 Cals. (1739 J.)

480 g. cooked cod or other white fish	
360 g. mashed potatoes	250 ml. milk
90 g. butter or margarine	1 tablespoon
120 g. tomatoes	chopped parsley
30 g. flour	seasoning

> Make a roux with two-thirds of the butter

and all the flour. Add milk gradually, bring to boil and stir over low heat until the sauce thickens.

Remove skin and bones, and flake fish.

Skin and dice tomatoes and add with the fish to the sauce.

Add parsley and season.

Put mixture in oven-proof dish, spread with the mashed potato and dot with remaining butter.

Bake at 375° F (Mark 4) for 30 minutes.

Baked Haddock with Peppers

Each serving Negligible C. 215 Cals. (901 J.)

720 g. fresh haddock	60 g. onion (1 small)
60 g. grated Cheddar cheese	30 g. green pepper seasoning

> Remove skin and bones from fish and cut into four pieces. Put in greased oven-proof dish.

De-seed and slice peppers, peel and slice onions and place on fish.

Cover and bake at 275° F (Mark ½) for 45 minutes

Before serving, remove from oven and sprinkle with cheese. Either turn up heat and brown in oven for 5 minutes or put under hot grill until cheese is browned.

Haddock Meringue

Each serving 10 C. 385 Cals. (1613 J.)

720 g. cooked fresh haddock	3 eggs
45 g. butter or margarine	100 ml. milk
240 g. mashed potatoes	dried thyme
	seasoning

> Separate eggs and beat 2 of the yolks with the milk into the potatoes.

Soften butter, add thyme and seasoning and blend into the potato mixture.

Remove skin and bones and flake fish. Mix in to potato mixture.

Put in pie dish and bake at 350° F (Mark 3) for 30 minutes. Remove from oven.

Whisk egg whites until stiff and fold in remaining yolk, spread over the fish, return to oven and bake for a further 15 minutes.

Haddock Mousse

Each serving Nil C. 265 Cals. (1110 J.)

240 g. fresh haddock	50 ml. tomato purée
3 egg yolks	15 g. gelatine
2 egg whites	lemon slices
125 ml. double cream	seasoning
125 ml. water	

> Remove skin and bones and put fish in pan with the water, bring to boil and simmer until tender. Drain, retaining liquor.

Flake haddock.

Dissolve gelatine in cooking liquor and mix with fish. Add tomato purée. Cool.

Separate eggs, beat yolks and blend into fish mixture.

Whip cream and fold in. Season to taste.

Whisk egg whites until stiff, fold in and spoon mixture into greased soufflé dish.

Chill in refrigerator.

Haddock in Mushroom Sauce

Each serving 7 C. Nil Cals. (1110 J.)

960 g. fresh haddock	250 ml. water
30 g. flour	juice of 1 lemon
30 g. butter or margarine	15 g. mustard
60 g. onion (1 small)	powder
120 g. mushrooms	chopped parsley
25 ml. wine vinegar	seasoning

> Remove skin and bones and place fish in oven-proof dish.

Wash, peel and chop mushrooms.

Make a roux with butter and flour, add water gradually, bring to boil and stir over low heat until sauce thickens.

Add mushrooms, vinegar, lemon juice, mustard, parsley and seasoning to sauce and bring back to boil.

Pour over fish and bake at 350° F (Mark 3) for 40 minutes.

Haddock Portugaise

Each serving Negligible C. 250 Cals. (1048 J.)

720 g. fresh haddock	120 g. tomatoes
30 g. butter or margarine	120 g. onion
30 g. grated Cheddar	(1 large)
cheese	seasoning

> Remove skin and bones and cut fish into four.

Place in greased oven-proof dish.

Peel and slice onion and tomato thinly and place evenly over the haddock.

Sprinkle with grated cheese and dot with butter.

Bake at 375° F (Mark 4) for 25 minutes.

Haddock and Tomato

Each serving 10 C. 310 Cals. (1299 J.)

960 g. fresh haddock fillets	60 g. onion (1 small)
50 ml. oil	240 g. tomatoes
30 g. flour	seasoning

> Remove skin and bones and place fish in oven-proof dish. Season, sprinkle with flour and pour on half the oil.

Peel and chop onion and tomatoes and cook gently in remaining oil for 10 minutes

Spread onion and tomato mixture over fish and bake at 350° F (Mark 3) for 30 minutes.

Hake Pudding

Each serving 5 C. 435 Cals. (1823 J.)

1 kg. hake	75 ml. single cream
2 eggs	mixed herbs
30 g. flour	seasoning
60 g. butter or margarine	

> Remove skin and bones and put fish through mincer.

Make a roux with butter and flour, remove from heat and stir in cream.

Separate eggs and beat yolks into the sauce. Add fish, herbs and seasoning.

Whisk whites until stiff and fold into mixture.

Pour into greased oven-proof dish, cover and bake at 375° F (Mark 4) for 45 minutes.

Halibut and Bacon

Each serving Negligible C. 350 Cals. (1467 J.)

1 kg. halibut	1 teaspoon wine vinegar
120 g. tomatoes	100 ml. water
120 g. streaky bacon	seasoning
120 g. onion (1 large)	

> Peel and chop onion and peel and slice tomatoes.

Remove skin and bones from fish.

Remove rind from bacon and chop finely. Put in pan and cook slowly for a few moments, add onions and fry in the bacon fat until these are transparent.

Add tomato slices and cook for a further few minutes

Season and place half the mixture in oven-proof dish.

Add halibut and top with another layer of the bacon mixture.

Pour on the vinegar and water and bake at 350° F (Mark 3) for 1 hour.

Halibut Mousse

Each serving Negligible C. 400 Cals. (1676 J.)

780 g. halibut	30 g. gelatine
200 ml. double cream	1 lemon
60 g. carrots	500 ml. water
60 g. onion (1 small)	bayleaf
90 g. cucumber	seasoning

> Remove skin and bones and place fish in large pan with the water.

Peel and dice carrots and onion and add, with bayleaf and seasoning, to the pan. Bring to boil and simmer for 15 minutes.

Remove fish and set aside, discard bayleaf and continue cooking vegetables for a further 15 minutes.

Flake fish, add to mixture and rub through sieve or purée in electric blender.

Dissolve gelatine in a little water and add with lemon juice and seasoning to the fish and vegetable purée. Allow to cool.

Whip cream until stiff and fold in.

Pour into soufflé dish and chill.

Serve garnished with thinly sliced cucumber.

Poached Halibut

Each serving Nil C. 265 Cals. (1110 J.)

1 kg. halibut or other white fish	water
30 g. butter or margarine	seasoning
lemon slices	

> Remove skin and bones and cut fish into four.

Put fish in pan with enough water to come half way up the fish. Add butter and seasoning.

Bring to boil and simmer gently until the fish is cooked (approximately 15 minutes).

Serve garnished with lemon slices.

Baked Herrings

Each serving 15 C. 600 Cals. (2514 J.)

1 kg. herrings (4 fish)	25 ml. vinegar
	50 ml. water

30 g. sugar	pinch ground cloves
60 g. soft breadcrumbs	seasoning

> Fillet fish, rub inside with salt and place in oven-proof dish.

Mix vinegar, sugar, cloves, seasoning and water together and pour over the herrings.

Sprinkle with breadcrumbs and bake at 375° F (Mark 4) for 30 minutes.

Herrings with Mustard Sauce

Each serving Nil C. 435 Cals. (1823 J.)

1 kg. herrings (4 fish)	squeeze lemon juice
90 g. butter or margarine	seasoning
2 teaspoons made mustard	

> Slit herrings along belly, turn on to clean working surface. Press firmly along backbone to loosen, then lift spine away.

Cream butter until soft and beat in mustard, lemon juice and seasoning. Spread mixture over the inside of the fish and close.

Wrap each herring in greased foil and place on baking tray.

Bake at 375° F (Mark 4) for 25 to 30 minutes.

Unwrap foil, pour cooking juices over the fish and serve hot.

Kedgeree

Each serving 10 C. 270 Cals. (1131 J.)

480 g. smoked haddock	60 g. butter or margarine

150 g. cooked long-grain
   rice
2 hard boiled eggs

chopped parsley
seasoning

> Flake fish and chop eggs.
  Melt butter, add fish, rice, egg and seasoning.
  Heat thoroughly over low heat.
  Sprinkle with parsley and serve.

Kipper with Cheese

Each serving Nil C. 340 Cals. (1425 J.)

480 g. kipper fillets
120 g. tomatoes

90 g. Cheddar cheese
black pepper

> Slice cheese thinly. Skin and slice tomatoes
  Grill fillets for 5 minutes.
  Cover with cheese slices and top with sliced
tomatoes.
  Return to grill for a further 5 minutes,
sprinkle with ground black pepper and serve
hot.

Kipper with Egg

Each serving 15 C. 245 Cals. (1027 J.)

240 g. kipper fillets
2 eggs
120 g. bread (4 slices)

25 ml. milk
black pepper

> Put kippers in boiling water and cook until
tender. Drain, flake and keep hot.
  Beat eggs with the milk, add flaked kipper
and scramble the mixture.
  Toast bread, spread with egg mixture and
sprinkle with ground pepper.

Kipper Paté

Each serving Nil C. 265 Cals. (1110 J.)

150 g. kipper fillets
90 g. butter or
  margarine
yolk of 1 hard boiled
  egg

juice of $\frac{1}{2}$ lemon
$\frac{1}{2}$ clove garlic
  crushed (if liked)
ground black pepper

> Cook kipper fillets in boiling water for
2 minutes.
  Drain and remove skin and as many bones as
possible.
  Pound to a pulp.
  Mash egg yolk with softened butter, lemon
juice and garlic.
  Blend egg mixture with the fish and season
with pepper.
  Serve as desired.

Baked Mackerel

Each serving Negligible C. 530 Cals. (2221 J.)

1 kg. mackerel (4 fish)
120 g. tomatoes
30 g. butter or margarine

lemon slices
chopped parsley
seasoning

> Remove heads and tails from fish and clean.
  Peel and slice tomatoes, put slices on each
fish and sprinkle with parsley and seasoning.
  Divide butter in four and dot each fish. Wrap
individually in greased foil and bake at 350° F
(Mark 3) for 30 minutes.
  Remove foil, pour on cooking juices and
serve garnished with lemon.

Savoury Mackerel

Each serving 15 C. 325 Cals. (1571 J.)

420 g. mackerel tinned in oil	1 teaspoon mixed herbs
4 thin slices bread (120 g.)	60 g. butter or margarine
120 g. grated Cheddar cheese	seasoning

> Drain and discard oil from tin.
  Remove skin and bones and mash fish with herbs. Season to taste
  Toast bread lightly and spread with butter.
  Divide mackerel into four and place on toast.
  Sprinkle with cheese and brown under hot grill.

Plaice Meunière

Each serving Nil C. 400 Cals.(1676 J.)

1 kg. plaice (4 whole fish)	juice 1 lemon chopped parsley
120 g. butter	seasoning

> Clean fish and fry in butter. When cooked, remove from pan, set aside and keep hot.
  Add lemon juice and seasoning to butter in pan and cook until golden brown.
  Pour juices over fish, sprinkle with parsley and serve.

Plaice with Orange

Each serving Negligible C. 296 Cals. (1164 J.)

720 g. plaice fillets (skinned)	30 g. butter or margarine
120 g. grated Edam cheese	seasoning
120 g. peeled orange	

> Put fish in oven-proof dish and dot with butter. Season to taste.
  Slice orange into rings and divide evenly over the fillets.
  Sprinkle with grated cheese and bake at 350° F (Mark 3) for 20 minutes.

Creamed Salmon Flan

Each serving 10 C. 250 Cals. (1048 J.)

shortcrust pastry using 60 g. flour (80 g. made pastry)	120 g. mushrooms (prepared)
225 g. tinned red salmon	seasoning
100 ml. single cream	

> Make pastry in usual way and roll out to fit 7 inch sandwich tin.
  Flake salmon. Peel and chop mushrooms.
  Mix salmon with cream, mushrooms and seasoning.
  Spread mixture evenly in the pastry case and bake at 400° F (Mark 5) for 35 minutes.

Salmon Kedgeree

Each serving 20 C. 540 Cals. (2263 J.)

420 g. tinned salmon
120 g. raw
  long-grained rice
4 hard boiled eggs

60 g. butter or
  margarine
100 ml. double cream
seasoning

> Cook rice in boiling salted water until tender. Remove from heat, drain well, return to pan and add butter.

Drain salmon, remove any bones and flake.

Chop eggs roughly and add, with the salmon, to the rice.

Season, pour in cream, mix well and reheat. Serve in pre-heated dish.

Sardine Paté

Each serving Nil C. 265 Cals. (1110 J.)

120 g. sardines
  tinned in oil
85 g. cream cheese

1 teaspoon lemon juice
½ teaspoon made mustard
pepper

> Drain off and discard oil. Remove spines and tails from sardines.

Using a wooden spoon, blend sardines thoroughly with cream cheese, lemon juice, mustard and pepper.

Chill and serve as desired.

Creamed Smoked Haddock

Each serving 10 C. 215 Cals. (901 J.)

240 g. smoked haddock
30 g. butter or margarine
30 g. flour
250 ml. milk

50 ml. single cream
1 egg
pinch mixed herbs
seasoning

> Simmer haddock in milk until cooked. Drain, reserving liquid.

Remove skin and bones and flake fish.

Make a roux with flour and butter, add reserved liquid gradually and stir over low heat until sauce thickens. Allow to cool.

Beat egg and stir into sauce, add fish, herbs and seasoning.

Return to heat and cook gently for a few minutes.

Just before serving stir in cream.

Smoked Haddock Pie

Each serving 10 C. 325 Cals. (1739 J.)

480 g. smoked haddock
240 g. spinach (frozen or
  prepared fresh)
240 g. tomatoes
4 hard boiled eggs
30 g. butter or margarine

250 ml. milk
30 g. flour
60 g. grated
  Cheddar cheese
seasoning

> Cook haddock in boiling water until tender. Drain, remove any skin and bones and flake.

Cook spinach, drain well, chop and put in oven-proof dish.

Peel and slice tomatoes and slice eggs.

Cover spinach with flaked fish, put a layer of egg slices and top with sliced tomatoes.

Make a roux with butter and flour, add milk

gradually and stir over low heat until sauce thickens. Stir in grated cheese reserving a little to sprinkle on top.

Season and pour sauce over other ingredients in the dish, sprinkle with remaining cheese.

Bake at 300° F (Mark 1) for 30 minutes.

Smoked Haddock Scallops

Each serving 10 C. 220 Cals. (922 J.)

480 g. smoked haddock	180 g. tomatoes
250 ml. milk	30 g. grated
30 g. butter	Parmesan cheese
or margarine	60 g. onion (1 small)
30 g. flour	seasoning

> Cook haddock in boiling water, drain and flake removing any skin and bones.

Peel and dice onion and simmer in milk until tender. Drain, reserving liquid.

Peel and dice tomatoes.

Make a roux with flour and butter, gradually add milk drained from onions and stir over low heat until the sauce thickens.

Add fish, onion and tomato to the sauce and season.

Put in 4 individual oven-proof dishes, sprinkle with cheese and bake at 400° F (Mark 5) for 10 minutes.

Smoked Haddock with Tomato

Each serving 5 C. 300 Cals. (1257 J.)

1 kg. smoked haddock	45 g. butter or
250 ml. milk	margarine
360 g. tomatoes	seasoning

> Peel and slice tomatoes.

Remove skin and bones from fish, cut into pieces and place in buttered oven-proof dish.

Top with tomato slices, pour on milk, dot with butter and season.

Bake at 350° F (Mark 3) for 30 minutes.

Baked White Fish

Each serving Nil C. 320 Cals. (1341 J.)

1 kg. white fish	slices lemon
(in one piece)	seasoning
50 ml. cooking oil	

> Wash fish. Leave skin and bone on.

Brush with oil and season.

Wrap in foil and bake at 350° F (Mark 3) for 1 to 1½ hours.

Remove foil, pour cooking juices over fish and serve garnished with lemon slices.

Poached White Fish

Each serving 5 C. 295 Cals. (1236 J.)

1 kg. cod or other white fish fillets	
30 g. carrots	25 ml. wine vinegar

30 g. onion (½ small) 750 ml. water
30 g. flour mixed herbs
30 g. butter or margarine seasoning

> Skin fish, remove bones and cut into four.
Peel and dice carrots and onions and put them in saucepan with water, vinegar, mixed herbs and seasoning.
Add fish, bring to boil and simmer for 10 to 15 minutes until fish is cooked.
Remove fish from pan and set aside keeping hot.
Return pan to heat and cook vegetables for a further 15 minutes.
Remove from heat, and rub through sieve or make thin purée in electric blender.
Make a roux with butter and flour, add the purée gradually and stir over a low heat until sauce thickens.
Pour over fish and serve.

Steamed White Fish Fillets

Each serving Nil C. 300 Cals. (1257 J.)

1 kg. plaice or any other white fish fillets
60 g. butter or margarine seasoning
lemon juice

> Remove skin and bones from fish.
Put on large oven-proof plate with butter, squeeze of lemon juice and seasoning. Cover with another oven-proof plate and place over pan of boiling water on low heat.
Cook for 15 to 20 minutes until fish is cooked.

Whiting in Mustard Sauce

Each serving Negligible C. 310 Cals. (1299 J.)

960 g. whiting 15 g. mustard powder
120 g. onion (1 large) juice ½ lemon
100 ml. dry white wine chopped parsley
30 g. butter or seasoning
  margarine

> Remove skin and bones from whiting and put in oven-proof dish.
Mix mustard powder, wine, lemon juice and seasoning together and pour over fish.
Dot with butter and bake at 350° F (Mark 3) for 15 to 20 minutes.
Before serving, sprinkle with parsley.

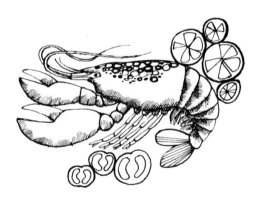

Whiting in Sauce

Each serving 5 C. 425 Cals. (1781 J.)

720 g. whiting (4 fillets) 30 g. flour

90 g. bacon
30 g. grated Cheddar
   cheese
1 green pepper

30 g. butter or
   margarine
250 ml. milk
seasoning

> Remove any skin and bones from fish, place in greased oven-proof dish and bake at 350° F (Mark 3) for 15 minutes.

Remove rind and chop bacon, peel and chop onion, de-seed and chop pepper.

Melt butter in pan, add bacon, onion and pepper. Fry until the onion is transparent.

Blend in flour and cook for a further minute or two.

Add milk gradually and stir over low heat until mixture thickens. Season to taste.

Pour sauce over fish, sprinkle with cheese, return to oven and bake for a further 20 minutes.

Meat

Each recipe makes four servings except where otherwise stated

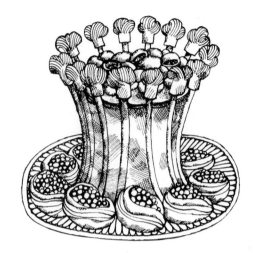

Boiled Bacon or Ham

Each serving Negligible C. 785 Cals. (3290 J.)

1 kg. piece of bacon or ham (boned)	peppercorns
30 g. dry brown breadcrumbs whole cloves	bay leaf water

> Soak joint in cold water overnight.

Remove, stick with cloves and place in large saucepan with fresh water, peppercorns and bay leaf.

Cover, bring to boil, skim and simmer for 1¼ hours.

To test if cooked, see if rind will come away easily. If so it is done and can be drained and left to cool.

Remove cloves, skin and excess fat and coat with breadcrumbs.

Boiled Beef and Carrots

Each serving 5 C. 390 Cals. (1684 J.)

1 kg. salt silverside	360 g. button onions
360 g. young carrots	pepper

> Soak silverside in water overnight.

Scrub and trim carrots and onions leaving them whole.

Drain meat from liquid and place in large pan with onions, carrots and pepper.

Just cover with water, bring to boil and simmer for 1¾ hours.

Drain and serve with vegetables.

Braised Beef

Each serving 10 C. 515 Cals. (2154 J.)

960 g. braising steak	brown stock (see recipe) or water
15 g. lard	1 tablespoon chopped parsley
240 g. onions (3 medium)	pinch dried thyme
240 g. carrots	seasoning
240 g. turnips	
30 g. celery	

> Cut meat into four.

Peel and dice onions, carrots and turnips. Trim and dice celery.

Heat lard and fry meat lightly. Transfer to oven-proof dish.

Fry vegetables until onion is transparent and add to the meat.

Add enough stock or water to come half way up the mixture in the dish.

Season to taste and add thyme and parsley.

Cover and cook at 325° F (Mark 2) for 2 hours.

Cold Beef Roll

Each serving 15 C. 546 Cals. (2288 J.)

480 g. fresh mince	2 eggs
240 g. lean bacon rashers	½ teaspoon grated
120 g. soft white	nutmeg
breadcrumbs	seasoning

> Trim and mince bacon and mix with meat and breadcrumbs.

Bind with beaten egg, add nutmeg and season to taste.

Put mixture in well oiled pudding basin large enough to allow for it to rise.

Cover with greaseproof paper or foil, place in saucepan containing enough boiling water to come half way up the basin.

Cook for 2 hours, refilling saucepan with boiling water from time to time as it evaporates.

Remove from water and leave contents in the basin in a cool place overnight.

Turn out and serve.

Piquant Beef Casserole

Each serving 10 C. 520 Cals. (2178 J.)

720 g. stewing steak (trimmed)	½ teaspoon curry powder
30 g. flour	50 ml. vegetable oil
180 g. onions (3 small)	25 ml. vinegar
120 g. mushrooms	1 teaspoon paprika
120 g. celery (trimmed)	garlic salt
500 ml. brown stock (see recipe) or water	seasoning

> Peel and dice onions and mushrooms and dice celery.

Cut meat into cubes and fry in heated oil until lightly browned. Transfer to oven-proof dish and add onions, mushrooms and celery.

Make a roux with flour and remaining oil in frying pan, blend in curry powder, paprika, vinegar and garlic salt. Add stock gradually stirring over low heat until sauce thickens.

Add any further seasoning to taste and pour sauce over meat and vegetables.

Cover and cook at 350° F (Mark 3) for 2 hours.

Savoury Beef Casserole

Each serving Negligible C. 300 Cals. (1257 J.)

720 g. stewing beef (trimmed)	½ teaspoon paprika
180 g. onions (3 small)	25 ml. Worcester sauce
120 g. tomatoes	25 ml. vinegar

60 g. courgettes
250 g. brown stock (see recipe) or water
½ teaspoon curry powder

mixed herbs
garlic salt
seasoning

> Dice beef and fry in its own fat over gentle heat until lightly browned. Transfer to oven-proof dish.

Peel and dice onions and tomatoes and add to the beef.

Slice but do not peel courgettes and add to mixture.

Mix stock or water with curry powder, paprika, Worcester sauce, vinegar, herbs, garlic salt and seasoning and pour over the meat and vegetables.

Cover and cook at 350° F (Mark 3) for 2½ hours.

Beef Stew with Wine

Each serving 5 C. 600 Cals. (2514 J.)

720 g. stewing steak (trimmed)
30 g. flour
60 g. bacon rashers
180 g. onions (3 small)
180 g. tomatoes

125 ml. dry white or red wine
50 ml. cooking oil
mixed herbs
125 ml. water
seasoning

> Peel and dice onions and tomatoes.

Cut meat into strips. Trim and chop bacon and fry with meat in heated oil until meat is slightly browned. Transfer to large saucepan.

Make roux with oil remaining in frying pan and flour, add water gradually, and stir over low heat until it thickens.

Pour over meat and bacon. Add onions, carrots, tomatoes, mixed herbs and seasoning.

Pour on wine, cover, bring to boil and simmer for 1½ to 2 hours.

Cauliflower Meat Pie

Each serving 10 C. 455 Cals. (1906 J.)

720 g. fresh minced beef
120 g. onion (1 large)
1 meat stock cube
120 g. tinned tomatoes
15 g. cornflour
480 g. cauliflower
125 ml. milk

250 ml. water
60 g. grated Cheddar cheese
10 ml. Worcester sauce
seasoning

> Peel and dice onion and put, with meat, in large saucepan.

Fry for 10 minutes slowly in their own juices. Remove from heat and drain off any surplus fat.

Dissolve stock cube in water and add, with tomatoes, Worcester sauce and seasoning, to meat.

Make a paste with cornflour and a little water and add to the saucepan.

Bring to boil and simmer for 20 minutes stirring from time to time. Transfer to oven-proof dish and keep hot.

Meanwhile remove outer leaves from cauliflower and break into pieces. Cook in boiling salted water until soft.

Strain, mash with a fork and stir in milk. Season to taste.

Spread cauliflower over the mince mixture, sprinkle with grated cheese and brown under hot grill.

Corned Beef Hash

Each serving 20 C. 560 Cals. (1928 J.)

360 g. corned beef	120 g. onion
480 g. mashed potato	(1 large)
1 egg	50 ml. cooking oil
30 g. butter or margarine	seasoning

> Peel and dice onion and fry in heated oil until transparent.

Dice corned beef.

Blend potato with butter, corned beef, onion, egg and seasoning.

Bake in shallow oven-proof dish at 350° F (Mark 3) for 20 to 25 minutes.

Cornish Pasties

Each serving 25 C. 245 Cals. (1027 J.)

shortcrust pastry using 120 g. flour	
(80 g. made pastry)	
240 g. stewing beef (trimmed)	1 egg
120 g. potato (raw)	seasoning
120 g. onions (raw) (2 small)	

> Make pastry in usual way, roll out thinly and cut into four large rounds.

Dice meat, peel and dice onion and potato and mix together, season and put a quarter of mixture on each pastry round.

Brush edges of pastry with beaten egg, fold and flute together with fingers.

Brush pasties with egg and bake at 375° F (Mark 4) for 15 minutes then lower

temperature to 300° F (Mark 1) for a further 45 minutes.

Danish Hash

Each serving 25 C. 400 Cals. (1676 J.)

600 g. potatoes (peeled)	4 eggs
240 g. onions (2 large)	2 teaspoons
360 g. cooked meat (diced)	Worcester sauce
60 g. butter or margarine	seasoning

> Dice potatoes and dry in clean cloth.

Peel and slice onions finely.

Using two frying pans, melt three quarters of the butter in one and fry potatoes until golden brown.

Put remaining butter in second pan and fry onions until lightly browned. Transfer to potato pan, add meat and Worcester sauce, season and fry until the meat is well heated.

Meanwhile fry eggs in onion pan.

Divide meat mixture into four and top each with fried egg.

Danish Pork

Each serving 10 C. 395 Cals. (1655 J.)

1 kg. white cabbage (whole)	peppercorns
1 kg. joint spareribs pork	water
60 g. butter	salt

> Remove outer leaves from cabbage, wash and drain, cut in quarters and shred.

Melt butter in large saucepan and fry joint turning to ensure that all sides are lightly browned. Remove from pan and set aside.

Cook shredded cabbage in the hot fat keeping it turning until the bulk has reduced and it has softened.

Return joint to cabbage in the pan, add peppercorns and salt to taste, barely cover with water. Bring to boil and simmer for $1\frac{1}{2}$ to 2 hours.

Serve meat on a bed of the cabbage.

Chicken Casserole

Each serving 5 C. 480 Cals. (2011 J.)

1 kg. chicken pieces	375 ml. chicken stock
30 g. flour	(see recipe)
60 g. butter or	125 ml. single cream
margarine	1 teaspoon dried
240 g. mushrooms	thyme
240 g. onions	seasoning
(2 large)	

> Sift flour with seasoning and dried thyme.

Skin chicken pieces and roll in flour, making sure all the flour is used.

Peel and slice mushrooms and onions.

Melt butter in large pan and fry chicken gently until golden brown. Transfer to oven-proof dish. Add mushrooms and onions.

Add stock gradually to cooking juices in pan, bring to boil and stir over low heat until it thickens.

Pour over chicken, cover and cook at 350°F (Mark 3) for approximately $1\frac{1}{2}$ hours.

Just before serving, stir in cream.

Quick Chicken Curry

Each serving 15 C. 235 Cals. (985 J.)

360 g. cooked chicken	30 g. seedless raisins
120 g. onion (1 large)	375 ml. chicken stock
120 g. apple	(see recipe)
30 g. flour	25 ml. cooking oil
3 teaspoons curry	squeeze lemon juice
powder	garlic salt

> Peel and chop onion finely. Peel and core apple. Dice chicken.

Wash raisins.

Heat oil in large saucepan and fry onion until transparent.

Blend in curry powder and flour and cook gently for a minute or two.

Add stock gradually and stir over low heat until it thickens.

Add apple and simmer for 15 minutes.

Mix in chicken and raisins, season with garlic salt to taste and return to heat.

Simmer for a further 15 minutes and just before serving, add a squeeze of lemon juice.

Corned Beef and Cheese Pie

Each serving 20 C. 555 Cals. (2325 J.)

480 g. corned beef	240 g. tomatoes
120 g. grated Cheddar	120 g. onion (1 large)
cheese	60 g. margarine
360 g. potatoes (peeled)	2 teaspoons meat
120 g. carrots	extract
60 g. peas	250 ml. water

120 g. mushrooms   seasoning

> Cook potatoes in boiling salted water until tender, mash them while still hot and blend in cheese.

Peel and dice carrots, onions, mushrooms and tomatoes.

Cook carrots, onions and peas in water until tender. Drain.

Melt margarine and fry diced corned beef, tomatoes and mushrooms.

Add carrots, onions and peas and fry for a further few minutes.

Put mixture in oven-proof dish, add meat extract mixed with boiling water and season to taste, bake for 15 minutes at 375° F (Mark 4).

Top with mashed potatoes and reheat in oven or brown under grill.

Chicory, Ham and Chicken Savoury

Each serving 5 C. 310 Cals. (1299 J.)

4 large chicory heads	30 g. flour
120 g. ham (4 slices)	120 g. grated
60 g. button mushrooms	Cheddar cheese
120 g. diced cooked	250 ml. chicken
chicken	stock (see recipe)
30 g. butter or margarine	seasoning

> Cook chicory heads in salted boiling water for 10 minutes.

Drain well.

Wrap a slice of ham round each celery head and put into oven-proof dish.

Wash and slice mushrooms and add, with chicken, to dish.

Make a roux with butter and flour, add stock gradually, bring to boil and stir over low heat until sauce thickens. Stir three-quarters of cheese into the sauce and cook until well blended. Season to taste.

Pour sauce over the wrapped chicory heads, sprinkle remaining cheese on top and bake for 25 to 30 minutes at 375° F (Mark 4).

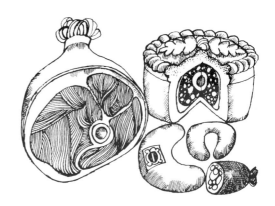

Dumplings

8 dumplings. Each 10 C. 115 Cals. (482 J.)

120 g. self-raising flour	water to mix
60 g. shredded suet	salt

> Rub flour and suet together.

Mix to a sticky dough with water and roll out by hand.

Divide into 8 dumplings.

Cover and cook in boiling stock for 20 minutes, or add to stew 20 minutes before serving.

Goulash

Each serving 10 C. 345 Cals. (1446 J.)

720 g. lean stewing steak (trimmed)	30 g. flour
30 g. lard	1 clove garlic
240 g. onions (2 large)	1 tablespoon paprika
1 red pepper	135 ml. plain yoghourt
1 green pepper	500 ml. water
120 g. tomatoes	seasoning

> Cut meat into cubes. Peel and dice onions and tomatoes.

De-seed and slice peppers.

Melt lard and fry meat until lightly browned. Transfer to large saucepan with onions, tomatoes and peppers.

Make roux with remaining fat in pan and flour, add water gradually and stir over low heat until the sauce thickens. Pour over meat and vegetables.

Crush garlic and add, with paprika, to meat. Season to taste.

Bring to boil and simmer for 1½ hours.

Just before serving stir in yoghourt.

Greek Shepherd's Pie

Each serving 25 C. 560 Cals. (1928 J.)

480 g. fresh minced beef	1 egg
180 g. onions (3 small)	125 ml. milk
360 g. potatoes	125 ml. water
240 g. tomatoes	50 ml. vegetable oil
30 g. butter or margarine	

30 g. flour	mixed herbs
30 g. grated Cheddar cheese	seasoning

> Peel and slice onions, tomatoes and potatoes.

Heat oil and cook onions until transparent. Remove from pan and set aside.

Fry potatoes for a few minutes but do not brown.

Make a roux with butter and flour, gradually add milk and water, bring to boil and stir over low heat until sauce thickens. Blend in cheese.

Remove from heat and add well beaten egg, herbs and seasoning.

Put a layer of potato in base of oven-proof dish, then alternate layers of mince, tomatoes, and onions. Continue until all ingredients are used ending with a layer of potato.

Between each layer put a little sauce leaving enough to coat the top.

Bake at 350° F (Mark 3) for 1½ hours.

Ham and Egg Mould

Each serving Negligible C. 170 Cals. (712 J.)

4 hard boiled eggs	30 g. aspic jelly crystals
120 g. lean cooked ham	500 ml. water
60 g. carrots (cooked)	seasoning
60 g. peas (cooked)	lettuce leaves
60 g. tomatoes (raw)	

> Heat a little of the water and dissolve aspic crystals, add remaining water and leave until beginning to set.

Dice carrots and tomatoes and mix with peas. Dice ham.

Season to taste.

Using a ring mould, pour in a little aspic to form a base and allow almost to set.

Cut eggs in half lengthwise and arrange so that the yolks show when turned out.

Add ham and vegetables in layers each separated by a layer of aspic.

Leave in cool place to set, turn out and serve on bed of lettuce.

Hamburgers

Each hamburger 5 C. 230 Cals. (964 J.)

360 g. lean fresh mince	1 egg
60 g. soft breadcrumbs	pinch of mixed herbs
60 g. onion (1 small)	oil for frying
50 ml. Worcester sauce	seasoning

> Peel and chop onion finely and mix with mince, breadcrumbs, herbs and seasoning.

Beat egg with Worcester sauce and bind the mince mixture.

Form into 8 flat cakes and fry in shallow hot fat for 10 minutes each side.

Ham Hash

Each serving 25 C. 555 Cals. (2325 J.)

360 g. lean cooked ham	480 g. potato
120 g. onions (1 large)	120 g. grated cheese
	60 g. margarine
60 g. carrots	2 meat stock cubes
1 green pepper	150 ml. water
	pinch of cayenne

120 g. baked beans pepper
50 ml. tomato purée

> Peel and mince onions and carrots.
Mince ham.
De-seed and chop pepper and fry in large saucepan, using half the margarine, until soft.

Add ham, onions and carrots and fry for a further 3 or 4 minutes.

Blend meat stock cubes with water and tomato purée and add to the pan with baked beans.

Season to taste and simmer in covered pan for 30 minutes.

Peel and cook potatoes until soft, mash with remaining margarine and mix in half the grated cheese.

Transfer ham mixture to oven-proof dish and top with potato mixture, sprinkle with remaining cheese and brown under hot grill.

Devilled Kidneys

Each serving 25 C. 410 Cals. (1718 J.)

480 g. kidneys (lamb or ox)	1 teaspoon curry powder
120 g. onion (1 large)	50 ml. cooking oil
120 g. tomatoes	250 ml. water
30 g. flour	lemon juice
480 g. potatoes (peeled)	paprika
1 egg	salt

> Skin kidneys, remove core and slice thinly.
Peel and slice onion and tomatoes.
Heat oil in large saucepan and brown kidneys gently. Add onion and cook until transparent.

Add tomatoes, blend in flour, add water gradually, bring to boil and stir over low heat until mixture thickens.

Blend in curry powder, paprika, lemon juice and salt to taste.

Cover pan and simmer for 1 hour.

Cook potatoes in boiling salted water until tender, drain, mash and beat in egg and butter.

Serve kidney mixture surrounded by ring of potato.

Crown Roast of Lamb

Each serving Negligible C. 960 Cals. (4022 J.)

2 pieces best end neck of lamb (12 chops)

240 g. button onions	60 g. butter or
240 g. button	margarine
mushrooms	dried rosemary
120 g. tomatoes	seasoning

> Ask your butcher to prepare a crown of lamb.

Sprinkle a little dried rosemary on inner side of chops.

Weigh and bake, allowing 20 minutes to the $\frac{1}{2}$ kg. plus 20 minutes over, at 375° F (Mark 4).

Before putting in oven, wrap top of each chop in foil to prevent burning during cooking.

Peel onions and leave whole. Peel and slice tomatoes. Wash mushrooms.

Put onions, mushrooms and tomatoes in oven-proof dish.

Add butter and seasoning and cook in covered dish in oven, with meat, for 1 hour.

Twenty minutes before cooking time for meat is completed, take meat out of oven, drain off fat and fill centre with mushroom mixture. Return to oven and cook for the final 20 minutes.

Before serving remove foil wrappings from chops.

Lamb Curry

Each serving 10 C. 315 Cals. (1320 J.)

300 g. cooked lamb	1½ dessertspoons
120 g. onion	curry powder
(1 large)	30 g. margarine
180 g. cooking apple	375 ml. brown stock
30 g. sultanas	(see recipe)
180 g. white cabbage	salt

> Dice lamb, shred cabbage and wash sultanas.

Peel and dice onion. Peel, core and dice apple.

Heat margarine in large saucepan and fry onion until transparent.

Add apple and cook for a further few minutes.

Add curry powder and stock and stir on low heat until well blended.

Add cabbage, sultanas and lamb.

Bring to boil, cover pan and simmer for 30 minutes.

Lambs' Hearts Stuffed

Each serving 10 C. 230 Cals. (964 J.)

4 small lambs' hearts	1 egg
(720 g.)	½ teaspoon dried sage
120 g. onion (1 large)	seasoning
60 g. soft breadcrumbs	

> Soak hearts in cold salted water for 30 minutes then remove central valve.

Peel onion and dice finely, mix with breadcrumbs, sage and seasoning. Bind with beaten egg.

Stuff each heart with a quarter of the mixture and wrap individually in lightly greased foil.

Bake at 400° F (Mark 5) for 1 to 1½ hours.

Lambs' Kidneys Braised

Each serving Negligible C. 250 Cals. (1048 J.)

480 g. lambs' kidneys	50 ml. cooking oil
120 g. onion (1 large)	250 ml. water
120 g. mushrooms	seasoning
120 g. tomatoes	

> Peel and slice tomatoes, onions and mushrooms.

Skin and core kidneys and cut in half lengthwise.

Brown kidneys in large saucepan in heated oil. Add onions and cook until transparent.

Add tomatoes, mushrooms, water and seasoning.

Cover pan, bring to boil and simmer for 1 hour.

Lamb Stew

Each serving 5 C. 615 Cals. (2572 J.)

720 g. stewing lamb	120 g. tomatoes
360 g. onions (3 large)	50 ml. cooking oil
120 g. turnips	500 ml. water
120 g. celery	seasoning

> Trim and dice celery and peel and dice other vegetables.

Cut meat into small pieces.

Heat oil in large saucepan and brown meat gently, add vegetables, water and seasoning.

Cover, bring to boil and simmer for 1½ to 2 hours.

Liver and Onions Braised

Each serving 10 C. 700 Cals. (2934 J.)

1 kg. ox liver	30 g. flour
120 g. bacon rashers	375 ml. brown stock
240 g. onions	(see recipe)
(2 large)	seasoning
60 g. butter or margarine	

> Trim rashers, slice liver and fry gently in melted butter. Transfer to oven-proof dish reserving fat.

Peel and cut onion into rings and add to the liver and bacon.

Make a roux with flour and fat in the pan, add stock gradually, bring to boil and stir over a low heat until the gravy thickens.

Season and pour over liver mixture.

Cook at 350° F (Mark 3) for 1 hour.

Liver and Rice Casserole

Each serving 15 C. 520 Cals. (2178 J.)

60 g. long grain rice (raw)	240 g. onions
720 g. calves' liver	(2 large)
240 g. lambs' kidney	250 ml. water
240 g. pork chipolata	seasoning
sausages	

> Wash rice and put in large oven-proof dish.
Slice liver. Peel and slice onion finely.
Skin and core kidneys and cut in half
lengthwise.
Put liver. kidneys, onions and sausages on
rice, pour on water and season.
Cover and cook at 350° F (Mark 3) for
1 hour.

Savoury Liver

Each serving 10 C. 275 Cals. (1152 J.)

360 g. lambs' liver	60 g. onion (1 small)
90 g. bacon	1 egg
60 g. soft	25 ml. Worcester sauce
breadcrumbs	chopped parsley
60 g. mushrooms	seasoning

> Slice liver and put in oven-proof dish.
Remove rind from bacon and trim excess
fat.
Peel and dice onion and mushrooms finely
and mix with soft breadcrumbs and parsley.
Bind with beaten egg and season.
Spread over the liver and top with bacon
slices.
Mix Worcester sauce with the water and
pour over liver and other ingredients.
Cover and bake at 350° F (Mark 3) for
1 hour.

Meat Loaf

Each serving 10 C. 320 Cals. (1341 J.)

480 g. fresh minced beef	1 egg
120 g. pork sausage	30 g. soft
meat	breadcrumbs
120 g. onion (1 large)	mixed herbs
120 g. tomato	seasoning

> Peel and dice finely onion and tomatoes.
Mix together mince, sausage meat, onion,
tomato, breadcrumbs, seasoning and herbs.
Bind with beaten egg.
Press into oiled bread tin, cover with foil and
bake at 350° F (Mark 3) for 1½ hours.
Turn out and serve hot or cold.

Mince in Batter

Each serving 20 C. 480 Cals. (2011 J.)

480 g. fresh mince	For batter:
120 g. onions (2 small)	120 g. self-raising flour
60 g. dripping	2 eggs
seasoning	water to mix

> Make batter. (See Yorkshire pudding recipe.)
Slice onions and fry in half the dripping
until golden brown.
Add mince to the pan and cook until the
meat is lightly browned. Season to taste.
Melt remaining dripping and pour it into an
oven-proof dish.
Add mince and onion mixture, pour on
batter and bake at 400° F (Mark 5) for 20 to
25 minutes until batter has risen and is golden
brown.

Boiled Mutton

Each serving 5 C. 300 Cals. (1257 J.)

1 kg. breast of mutton (rolled)   90 g. tomatoes
180 g. carrots   water
180 g. onions (3 small)   dried rosemary
90 g. turnips   seasoning

> Peel and chop roughly carrots, onions,
turnips and tomatoes.

Put in large saucepan with mutton, rosemary
and seasoning.

Add just enough water to cover.

Bring to boil and simmer in covered pan for
$1\frac{1}{2}$ to 2 hours.

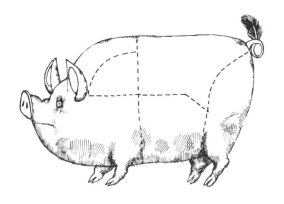

Oxtail Stew

Each serving 15 C. 460 Cals. (1927 J.)

1 oxtail ($1\frac{1}{2}$ kg.)   60 g. dripping
120 g. onion (1 large)   1 litre water
120 g. carrots   mixed herbs
120 g. turnips   seasoning
75 g. flour

> Joint oxtail and roll in flour.

Melt dripping in large saucepan, add oxtail
and fry gently until brown. Blend in any
remaining flour.

Peel and dice onion, carrots and turnips and
add to meat.

Add herbs, water and seasoning.

Bring to boil and simmer in covered pan for
2 to 3 hours until meat leaves the bone easily.

Boiled Ox Tongue

Each serving Nil C. 770 Cals. (3226 J.)

1 ox tongue (1 kg.)   mixed herbs
30 g. gelatine   seasoning

> Put tongue in large pan, cover with water
and add herbs and seasoning.

Bring to boil, skim and simmer in covered
pan for $2\frac{1}{2}$ to 3 hours.

Remove from pan, plunge tongue in cold
water, skin and trim off root.

Press into cake tin or soufflé dish.

Melt gelatine in 500 ml. of the cooking
liquor, pour over tongue, put weighted plate on
the mould and leave in cool place to set.

Turn out and serve.

Pork Chops with Peppers

Each serving Negligible C. 450 Cals. (1886 J.)

4 large lean pork chops   240 g. tomatoes
  (1 kg.)   175 ml. water
120 g. onion (1 large)   dried thyme
1 large green pepper   seasoning

> Peel tomatoes and cook in water until very tender. Rub through sieve or purée in electric blender. Season to taste.

Fry chops gently in own fat until lightly browned. Transfer to oven-proof dish.

Peel and cut onion into rings, de-seed and slice pepper and add to chops.

Add seasoning, dried thyme and tomato purée.

Cover and cook at 350° F (Mark 3) for 2 hours.

Pork Chops Piquant

Each serving 5 C. 415 Cals. (1739 J.)

4 lean pork chops (1 kg.)	30 g. butter
120 g. onions (1 large)	seasoning
120 g. cooking apple	

> Cut 4 pieces of foil big enough to wrap and place a chop in the centre of each.

Peel and slice onions. Peel, core and slice apple.

Top each chop with onion and apple slices, dot with butter, season and wrap in foil making sure that each parcel is well secured.

Bake at 375° F (Mark 4) for 1½ hours.

Remove foil before serving and pour cooking juices over chops.

Crown Roast of Pork

Each serving Negligible C. 510 Cals. (2176 J.)

2 pieces of pork ribs	60 g. butter or
(12 chops)	margarine

240 g. button mushrooms	dried thyme
240 g. tomatoes	seasoning

> Ask your butcher to prepare crown roast of pork.

Cover top of each chop with foil to prevent burning while cooking.

Weigh meat and roast, allowing 30 minutes to the ½ kg. plus 30 minutes over, at 425° F (Mark 6).

Peel and slice tomatoes. Wash mushrooms and leave whole.

Put mushrooms, tomatoes, butter, thyme and seasoning in oven-proof dish.

Cook in oven for 1 hour in covered dish.

Thirty minutes before cooking time for meat is completed, remove meat from oven and pour off excess fat.

Fill centre with tomato and mushroom mixture, return meat to oven and cook for the final 30 minutes.

Before serving remove foil wrapping from chops.

Pork Fillet in Pastry

Each serving 25 C. 390 Cals. (1634 J.)

shortcrust pastry using 120 g. flour	1 egg
(80 g. made pastry)	seasoning
480 g. pork fillet (trimmed)	

> Make pastry in usual way and roll out until just larger than pork fillet. Moisten edges with water.

Place fillet on pastry, season and roll the meat up in the pastry. Seal ends of pastry firmly.

Brush with beaten egg and prick top.

Bake at 300° F (Mark 1) for 1 hour.

Stewed Steak and Mushrooms

Each serving 5 C. 450 Cals. (1886 J.)

720 g. stewing steak (trimmed)	100 ml. milk
240 g. mushrooms	250 ml. water
30 g. margarine	seasoning
30 g. flour	

> Cut steak into cubes and fry in large saucepan in its own fat until lightly browned.

Make a roux with the margarine and flour, add milk and water gradually and stir over low heat until the sauce thickens.

Season sauce and pour over steak.

Cover, bring to boil and simmer for $1\frac{1}{2}$ hours.

Peel and dice mushrooms (including stalks) and add to the meat 20 minutes before cooking time is completed.

Swedish Meat Balls

8 meat balls, each 5 C. 220 Cals. (922 J.)

480 g. fresh mince	1 meat stock cube
60 g. soft breadcrumbs	1 litre water
30 g. mashed potatoes	50 ml. oil for
250 ml. milk	cooking
1 egg	$\frac{1}{2}$ teaspoon
$\frac{1}{2}$ teaspoon celery salt	nutmeg
$\frac{1}{2}$ teaspoon mustard powder	seasoning

> Beat egg with milk and pour over breadcrumbs.

Add mince, celery salt, mustard powder, nutmeg and seasoning, mix well and blend in potato to form a moist mixture.

Divide into 8 meat balls.

Heat oil and, when smoking, fry meat balls until brown.

Dissolve stock cube in water in large saucepan, bring to boil, add meat balls and simmer for 30 to 40 minutes.

Creamed Sweetbreads

Each serving 10 C. 505 Cals. (2112 J.)

760 g. sweetbreads	50 ml. single cream
500 ml. chicken stock	45 g. flour
(see recipe)	lemon slices
60 g. carrots	mixed herbs
60 g. onion (1 small)	chopped parsley
45 g. butter or margarine	seasoning

> Wash sweetbreads thoroughly and soak in cold water for 2 hours.

Drain, blanch in boiling water then plunge in cold.

Remove any fat and pipes and cut sweetbreads into pieces.

Peel and dice carrots and onions and put in large saucepan.

Add sweetbreads, stock, herbs and seasoning.

Bring to boil and simmer for $1\frac{1}{2}$ hours. Transfer sweetbreads and vegetables to serving dish and keep hot.

Make a roux with butter and flour, add cooking stock gradually and stir over low heat until the sauce thickens.

Cook for a few minutes, remove from heat, stir in cream and pour sauce over sweetbreads.

Serve garnished with lemon slices and chopped parsley.

Tinker's Casserole

Each serving 10 C. 355 Cals. (1487 J.)

480 g. stewing steak (trimmed)	25 ml. Worcester sauce
30 g. flour	120 g. mushrooms
120 g. streaky bacon	pinch of thyme
120 g. carrots	1 bay leaf
250 ml. light ale	seasoning

> Peel and slice carrots and mushrooms.

Cut meat into cubes and toss in seasoned flour.

Chop bacon and fry until the fat runs, add steak to the pan and fry until lightly browned. Blend in any remaining flour with a little of the ale.

Put meat and bacon, with their cooking juices, in oven-proof dish and add all remaining ingredients except mushrooms.

Cover and cook at 300°F (Mark 1) for 2 hours.

20 minutes before end of cooking time, add mushrooms.

Tripe and Onions

Each serving 10 C. 180 Cals. (754 J.)

480 g. prepared tripe	30 g. cornflour
125 ml. milk	125 ml. water
240 g. onions (2 large)	seasoning

> Cut tripe into cubes. Peel onions and slice into rings.

Put tripe, onions, milk, water and seasoning in large saucepan, cover, bring to boil and simmer for 1 to 1½ hours. Transfer tripe and onions to serving dish and keep hot.

Mix cornflour to a paste with a little cold water, gradually add the hot tripe stock and stir over low heat until the sauce thickens.

Pour sauce over the tripe and serve hot.

Veal in Tomato Sauce

Each serving 10 C. 300 Cals. (1257 J.)

480 g. stewing veal (trimmed)	240 g. tomatoes
60 g. butter or margarine	250 ml. water
30 g. flour	mixed herbs
120 g. onion (1 large)	seasoning

> Peel and dice tomatoes and onion.

Cut meat into 4 slices.

Cook tomatoes in water until very soft. Rub through sieve or purée in electric blender.

Heat half butter in frying pan and brown meat lightly.

Transfer to oven-proof dish and add onions.

Make a roux with flour, remaining butter and juices in frying pan, add tomato purée gradually and stir over low heat until it thickens.

Season, add herbs and pour tomato sauce over meat and onion.

Cover and cook at 300°F (Mark 1) for 1 hour.

Ragout of Veal

Each serving Negligible C. 275 Cals. (1152 J.)

720 g. stewing veal (trimmed)
120 g. onion (1 large)
240 g. tomatoes
120 g. mushrooms
50 ml. single cream

25 ml. cooking oil
500 ml. water
paprika
dried thyme
salt

> Dice veal.

Peel and dice tomatoes, onions and mushrooms.

Heat oil in large saucepan and brown veal lightly.

Add tomatoes, onions and water to the pan.

Season with paprika, dried thyme and salt.

Cover pan bring to boil and simmer for 1 hour.

20 minutes before end of cooking time, add mushrooms.

Just before serving, add cream.

Shepherd's Pie

Each serving 20 C. 280 Cals. (1173 J.)

360 g. fresh mince
480 g. potatoes (peeled)
60 g. onion (1 small)
30 g. carrots

15 g. butter or margarine
1 teaspoon mixed herbs
seasoning

> Cook potatoes in salted boiling water until tender, mash with fork, blend in butter and whisk.

Put mince in large saucepan and brown in its own fat on low heat.

Peel and dice onions and carrots and add to mince.

Put enough water to come half way up the mixture in the pan.

Add mixed herbs and seasoning, cover, bring to boil and simmer for ¾ to 1 hour.

Transfer mince to a pie dish, spread with mashed potatoes and cook at 350° F (Mark 3) for 30 minutes.

Braised Steak and Onions

Each serving 10 C. 420 Cals. (1760 J.)

720 g. braising steak (trimmed)
30 g. flour
180 g. onions (3 small)
120 g. carrots

50 ml. cooking oil
500 ml. brown stock (see recipe)
mixed herbs
seasoning

> Cut steak into four.

Peel and cut onions and carrots into rings.

Fry meat in heated oil until lightly browned and transfer to oven-proof dish.

Fry onions until transparent and add, with the carrots, to the meat.

Make a roux with flour and the cooking juices in the frying pan, add stock gradually and stir over low heat until it thickens. Season, add herbs and pour sauce over steak.

Cover and cook at 300° F (Mark 1) for 2 hours.

Steak and Kidney Pie

Each serving 20 C. 275 Cals. (1152 J.)

pastry using 120 g. flour (80 g. made pastry)
480 g. stewing steak (trimmed)

120 g. kidney
120 g. onion (1 large)
seasoning

> Core kidney. Cut steak and kidney into cubes.

Peel and slice onion and put, with meat, into large saucepan.

Season and add just enough water to cover the mixture.

Bring to boil and simmer in covered pan for 1 hour.

When cooked, transfer to pie dish.

Make pastry in usual manner, roll out and cover meat.

Bake at 350° F (Mark 3) for 30 minutes.

Stewed Steak and Kidneys

Each serving Negligible C. 400 Cals. (1676 J.)

480 g. stewing steak (trimmed)	50 ml. cooking oil
240 g. lambs' kidneys	1 litre water
180 g. onions (3 small)	mixed herbs
90 g. carrots	seasoning

> Peel and dice carrots and onions.

Core kidneys and cut these and the meat into cubes. Brown lightly in heated oil in large saucepan.

Add onions, carrots and water.

Season and add herbs.

Cover, bring to boil and simmer for 1½ to 2 hours.

Veal Chops with Rice

Each serving 15 C. 360 Cals. (1508 J.)

4 veal chops (720 g.)	125 ml. chicken stock (see recipe)
30 g. flour	

120 g. tomatoes	50 ml. cooking oil
360 g. onions (3 large)	60 g. stoned olives
60 g. cooked rice	garlic salt

> Sieve flour with garlic salt and toss chops in this making sure all flour is used.

Peel and chop tomatoes and onions.

Heat oil in large saucepan and brown chops lightly. Add tomatoes, onions and stock. Season to taste.

Cover pan, bring to boil and simmer for 45 minutes.

Remove chops and keep hot.

Add rice and olives to remaining ingredients in pan and cook for a few minutes until rice is thoroughly heated.

Transfer to heated serving dish and top with the chops.

Yorkshire Pudding

8 puddings each 5 C. 75 Cals. (314 J.)

75 g. plain flour	30 g. lard
1 egg	75 ml. water
50 ml. milk	seasoning

> Mix flour and seasoning.

Beat egg with milk and water, stir gradually into flour and beat until smooth and creamy.

Stand in cool place for at least an hour.

Divide lard between 8 patty pans and heat in oven until the fat is very hot, pour in batter and bake at 450° F (Mark 7) for 10 minutes.

Vegetables

Each recipe makes four servings, except where otherwise stated

Bubble and Squeak

Each serving 15 C. 235 Cals. (985 J.)

450 g. cooked potatoes
240 g. cooked cabbage
1 egg

50 ml. cooking oil
seasoning

> Mash potatoes and dice cabbage finely. Mix together, season and bind with beaten egg.
  Heat oil and fry potato mixture. When one side is brown, turn and brown other side.
  Serve hot.

Brussels Sprouts and Onions

Each serving Negligible C. 90 Cals. (377 J.)

720 g. brussels sprouts
00 g. onions (1 small)

30 g. butter
seasoning

> Trim sprouts and cook in boiling salted water until tender.
  Drain.
  Peel and slice onion and fry in the butter until transparent.
  Mix sprouts with onion, check for seasoning and fry for 2 minutes.

Dressed Cabbage

Each serving Negligible C. 90 Cals. (377 J.)

1 kg. savoy cabbage
30 g. butter
25 ml. vinegar

10 g. dry mustard
seasoning

> Remove and discard outer leaves and main stalk. Wash and shred remaining cabbage.
  Cook in a little salted boiling water until tender. Drain well.
  Soften butter and blend with mustard and vinegar. Pour over cabbage, toss thoroughly, and serve hot.

Dutch Cabbage

Each serving Negligible C. 140 Cals. (1006 J.)

1 kg. savoy cabbage	1 teaspoon carraway
60 g. butter or	seeds
margarine	water
	seasoning

> Remove and discard outer leaves and cut cabbage in four. Remove and discard stem and shred remaining cabbage finely.

Melt butter in large pan and toss cabbage in this with a spoon until well coated with butter. Cook for a few minutes until cabbage has reduced in bulk.

Add enough water to pan to come half way up the cabbage, season and add carraway seeds.

Cover and boil quickly for approximately 7 minutes.

Drain and serve hot.

Stuffed Cabbage

Each serving 10 C. 270 Cals. (1131 J.)

1 savoy cabbage (1 kg.)	60 g. bacon (raw)
250 ml. chicken stock	60 g. dry breadcrumbs
(see recipe)	dried thyme
240 g. pork (raw)	seasoning

> Remove and discard outer leaves, cut base of cabbage so that it stands upright. With a sharp knife scoop out centre, wash cabbage shell and put in oven-proof dish. (Reserve cabbage heart for future use.)

Mince together bacon and pork, add seasoning and thyme and fill centre of cabbage.

Pour stock over cabbage and sprinkle top with breadcrumbs.

Cover and bake at 350°F (Mark 3) for $1\frac{3}{4}$ hours

Carrots in Milk

Each serving 5 C. 155 Cals. (649 J.)

480 g. young carrots	chopped parsley
60 g. butter	seasoning
100 ml. milk	

> Scrape carrots, cut into thin rounds and put in oven-proof dish.

Add milk, butter and seasoning.

Cover and bake at 400°F (Mark 5) for 45 minutes.

Before serving, sprinkle with parsley.

Vichy Carrots

Each serving 5 C. 145 Cals. (566 J.)

480 g. young carrots	chopped parsley
60 g. butter	seasoning

> Scrape carrots and cut into matchstick pieces.

Melt butter in saucepan, add carrots and seasoning, cover and cook slowly until tender. (15 to 20 minutes.)

Transfer carrots with cooking juices to heated serving dish, and sprinkle with parsley before serving.

Cauliflower au Gratin

Each serving Negligible C. 200 Cals. (838 J.)

1 large cauliflower (1 kg.)	60 g. grated Cheddar cheese
60 g. butter or margarine	seasoning

> Remove and discard outer leaves and wash cauliflower, break into small pieces and cook in boiling salted water until tender.

Transfer to greased oven-proof dish, season to taste, sprinkle with grated cheese and dot with butter.

Brown under hot grill.

Cauliflower Cheese

Each serving 10 C. 545 Cals. (2284 J.)

1 large cauliflower	700 ml. milk
4 eggs	90 g. grated Cheddar cheese
120 g. butter or margarine	seasoning

> Remove and discard outer leaves and break remaining cauliflower into pieces. Cook in salted boiling water until tender. Drain, transfer to oven-proof dish and keep hot.

Put eggs, milk and butter in top of double saucepan over hot water. Cook gently whisking all the time until the mixture starts to thicken. (Make sure the water does not boil dry or sauce will curdle.)

Remove from heat and stir in most of the cheese. Season to taste.

Pour sauce over cauliflower, sprinkle with reserved cheese and brown under hot grill.

Cauliflower Soufflé

Each serving Negligible C. 135 Cals. (712 J.)

1 large cauliflower (1 kg.)	60 g. grated Cheddar cheese
15 g. butter	$\frac{1}{2}$ teaspoon made mustard
120 g. tomatoes	seasoning
25 ml. milk	

> Remove and discard outer leaves from cauliflower, cut in four and cook in salted boiling water until tender. Drain and transfer to greased large soufflé dish.

Skin and slice tomatoes and cook gently in butter for a few minutes. Allow to cool.

Separate eggs, and beat yolks and milk together. Mix in tomatoes and half the cheese. Season to taste.

Whisk egg whites until stiff and fold into mixture.

Spoon egg mixture on to cauliflower, sprinkle with remaining cheese and bake at 400°F (Mark 5) until cheese is melted and brown. (Approximately 10 minutes.)

Belgian Celery

Each serving Negligible C. 105 Cals. (440 J.)

480 g. celery (trimmed)	2 hard boiled eggs
75 ml. mayonnaise (see recipe)	1 tablespoon chopped parsley
25 ml. tomato sauce	

> Wash and cut celery into strips. Cook in boiling salted water until tender. Drain and cool. Transfer to serving dish.

Shell and chop eggs roughly.

Mix mayonnaise with tomato sauce and spread on celery.

Sprinkle with chopped egg and garnish with parsley.

Braised Celery

Each serving 10 C. 140 Cals. (587 J.)

1 kg. celery (trimmed)	30 g. flour
30 g. butter or	250 ml. stock or water
margarine	seasoning

> Wash celery and cut into short strips. Put into oven-proof dish.

Make a roux with butter and flour, add stock gradually and stir over low heat until sauce thickens.

Season and pour over celery. Cover and bake at 350° F (Mark 3) for 1 hour.

Braised Chicory

Each serving Negligible C. 105 Cals. (440 J.)

4 large chicory heads	squeeze of lemon juice
45 g. butter	seasoning

> Trim and wash chicory but leave heads whole.

Put chicory in ovenproof dish greased with a little of the butter, season and add lemon juice.

Dot with remaining butter, cover and bake at 375° F (Mark 4) for 30 minutes.

Coleslaw

Each serving 5 C. 175 Cals. (733 J.)

480 g. savoy cabbage	25 ml. white vinegar
60 g. carrots	50 ml. mayonnaise
30 g. celery (trimmed)	(see recipe)
25 ml. olive oil	seasoning

> Remove and discard outer leaves, wash cabbage and shred finely.

Scrape and grate carrots. Wash celery and dice finely.

Beat together oil, vinegar, mayonnaise and seasoning and mix with cabbage, carrot and celery.

Courgettes in Batter

15 fritters each 5 C. 60 Cals. (251 J.)

480 g. courgettes	125 ml. milk
1 egg	oil for frying
60 g. flour	seasoning

> Do not peel courgettes but wash them and slice into 15 pieces.

Make a thick batter (see Yorkshire pudding recipe) with egg, flour, milk and seasoning.

Dip each courgette in batter making sure that all the batter is used.

Fry in hot oil until golden brown. (Approximately 5 minutes).

Cucumber Salad

Each serving 5 C. 25 Cals. (105 J.)

480 g. cucumber	25 ml. lemon juice
15 g. sugar	1 tablespoon dried dill
1 tablespoon salt	white pepper
100 ml. white vinegar	

> Wash cucumbers and trim top and base.
Score by running fork down skin and cut cucumber into very thin slices.
Put in a dish with salt and stand in cool place for at least an hour, then drain well.
Mix together vinegar, sugar, pepper, lemon juice and dill.
Arrange cucumber slices on serving dish, pour on vinegar mixture and chill before serving.

Steamed Cucumber

Each serving Negligible C. 125 Cals. (524 J.)

480 g. cucumber	seasoning
60 g. butter	

> Peel and cut cucumber into thick rings.
Season and cook in top of double saucepan over boiling water for 20 minutes.
Drain and transfer to heated serving dish, dot with butter and serve.

Leeks au Gratin

Each serving Negligible C. 335 Cals. (1403 J.)

1 kg. leeks (trimmed)	125 ml. double cream
120 g. grated Cheddar cheese	seasoning

> Wash leeks well and leave whole. Cook in salted boiling water until tender.
Sprinkle half the cheese on base of lightly oiled oven-proof dish, add leeks, pour on cream and sprinkle with remaining cheese.
Cover and bake at 375°F (Mark 4) for 20 minutes.

Leek Pie

Each serving 20 C. 795 Cals. (3332 J.)

pastry using 90 g. flour (120 g. made shortcrust pastry)	250 ml. double cream
	2 eggs
300 g. leeks (trimmed)	120 g. lean bacon
60 g. butter	seasoning

> Make pastry in usual way.

Wash leeks well and put in pan with butter, cover and cook until tender but not brown.

Dice bacon, add to leeks and cook for a few minutes. Transfer to small pie dish.

Beat eggs and cream together and pour over leeks. Season to taste.

Roll out pastry and cover dish.

Bake at 350°F (Mark 3) for 30 minutes.

Leek Salad

Each serving Negligible C. 200 Cals. (838 J.)

1 kg. leeks (trimmed)	chopped parsley
160 ml. French dressing (see recipe)	seasoning

> Wash and cook leeks in boiling salted water until tender.

Drain well and transfer to shallow dish.

Pour on dressing and leave for 12 hours turning leeks from time to time.

Before serving, remove from dressing and roll in chopped parsley.

Glazed Onions

Each serving 5 C. 140 Cals. (587 J.)

480 g. button onions	250 ml. chicken stock (see recipe)
60 g. butter or margarine	seasoning

> Peel onions and leave whole.

Put stock, butter and seasoning in a

saucepan, bring to boil, add onions and simmer until onions are tender. (Approximately 30 minutes).

Transfer onions to serving dish and keep hot.

Boil liquid until it thickens and is reduced by at least half.

Pour over onions and serve hot.

Stuffed Onions

Each serving 20 C. 395 Cals. (1655 J.)

4 large onions (1 kg.)	120 g. tomatoes
180 g. fresh mince	500 ml. brown stock
60 g. bacon	(see recipe)
30 g. carrots	mixed herbs
60 g. mushrooms	seasoning
60 g. soft breadcrumbs	

> Peel onions and leave whole. Gently push out all the centre leaving thin outer shell. Trim base so that the shell stands upright. Place in oven-proof dish.

Mince bacon, carrots, mushrooms and onion centres, and add to fresh mince. Add breadcrumbs and mixed herbs.

Peel and dice tomatoes and add to mince mixture. Pour on stock, season to taste and mix well.

Fill onion cases with the mixture. (Any that will not fit into the onion shells can be put round them.)

Cover and bake at 350°F (Mark 3) for $1\frac{1}{2}$ hours.

Onion Tart

Each serving 25 C. 590 Cals. (2472 J.)

shortcrust pastry
   using 120 g. flour
300 g. onions
30 g. butter

250 ml. double cream
pinch of nutmeg
seasoning

> Make pastry in usual way but bind with one of the eggs instead of water. Roll out and line 8-inch flan tin.

Peel and chop onions finely and fry gently in butter until transparent.

Beat together remaining eggs, cream, nutmeg and seasoning and combine with onions.

Fill pastry flan with the mixture and bake at 375° F/Mark 4 for 30 to 40 minutes.

Peppers and Black Olive Salad

Each serving Negligible C. 745 Cals. (3123 J.)

120 g. green peppers
120 g. red peppers
120 g. black olives
   (stoned)
240 g. cream cheese
100 ml. wine vinegar

50 ml. dry sherry
20 ml. Worcester sauce
100 ml. olive oil
1 teaspoon salt
black pepper

> De-seed and wash peppers, slice finely and cook in boiling salted water for 4 minutes. Drain and leave to cool.

Mix together vinegar, sherry, Worcester sauce, oil, salt and black pepper and pour over the peppers.

Chill for several hours.

Just before serving, pour off half the liquid, add olives and mix in cheese.

Potato Cakes

14 cakes. Each 10 C. 135 Cals. (566 J.)

360 g. cooked potatoes
120 g. flour
90 g. grated Cheddar
   cheese

30 g. margarine
1 egg
oil for frying
seasoning

> Mash potatoes and blend in grated cheese.

Rub margarine into seasoned flour. Mix with potatoes and cheese and bind with beaten egg.

Roll out on a pastry board to approximately $\frac{1}{4}$-inch thickness and cut into 14 cakes.

Fry in heated oil until golden brown. (Approximately 3 minutes each side.)

Potato Croquettes

12 Croquettes. Each 10 C. 95 Cals. (398 J.)

480 g. cooked potatoes
45 g. butter or
   margarine
2 eggs

60 g. dry breadcrumbs
oil for frying
seasoning

> Mash potatoes, blend in butter and seasoning and bind with one egg.

Divide into 12 small croquettes, beat remaining egg, dip each croquette in egg and roll in breadcrumbs. Re-dip in egg and breadcrumbs to ensure all surfaces are well covered.

Fry in hot oil until golden brown.

Cheese Jacket Potatoes

Each serving 20 C. 310 Cals. (1299 J.)

4 medium sized old potatoes (480 g.)	90 g. grated Cheddar cheese
60 g. butter or margarine	seasoning

> Wash potatoes, prick skins with a fork and bake at 350° F (Mark 3) until tender. (Approximately 1 hour.)

Cut potatoes in half, scoop out centre and blend this with butter and two-thirds of the cheese. Season and return to skins.

Sprinkle remaining cheese over potato halves and brown under hot grill.

Stuffed Jacket Potatoes

Each serving 20 C. 160 Cals. (670 J.)

4 medium-sized old potatoes (480 g.)	30 g. butter or margarine
120 g. mushrooms	seasoning
60 g. onions (1 small)	

> Wash potatoes, prick skins with a fork and bake at 350° F (Mark 3) until tender. (Approximately 1 hour.)

Peel and dice finely mushrooms and onions. Fry in butter until cooked.

Cut potatoes in half, scoop out centre and mash with a fork.

Mix with mushrooms and onions, season and return to potato skins.

Reheat in oven before serving.

New Potato Salad

Each serving 20 C. 150 Cals. (628 J.)

480 g. new potatoes	1 tablespoon chopped chives
60 g. spring onions	25 ml. olive oil
1 tablespoon chopped parsley	25 ml. wine vinegar seasoning

> Scrub potatoes and cook in skin in boiling salted water until tender. Drain, allow to cool and remove skin.

Trim and wash spring onions and chop finely.

Dice potatoes and mix well with onions, parsley, chives, oil and vinegar.

Serve chilled.

Potato Tart

Each serving 20 C. 280 Cals. (1173 J.)

300 g. cooked potatoes	2 eggs
30 g. flour	120 g. lean bacon
30 g. butter	30 g. grated cheese
135 ml. milk	seasoning

> Mash potatoes and blend in flour and butter. Roll out on pastry board to about ¾ inch thickness.

Line an 8-inch flan tin with the potato pastry and bake at 400° F (Mark 5) for 15 minutes. Remove from oven.

Chop bacon and spread on base of potato flan.

Beat eggs and milk together, season and pour over bacon.

Sprinkle with grated cheese and return to oven. Bake for a further 25 minutes.

Special Creamed Potatoes

Each serving 20 C. 260 Cals. (1089 J.)

480 g. old potatoes	½ teaspoon thyme
2 eggs	seasoning
60 g. butter or	
margarine	

> Peel and dice potatoes and boil in salted water until very soft. Drain.

Mash potatoes roughly and blend in butter.

Beat eggs and whisk into the potatoes until the mixture becomes pale and creamy.

Add thyme and season to taste. Transfer to oven-proof dish.

Bake at 300° F (Mark 1) for 45 minutes.

Before serving, brown for a few minutes under hot grill.

Ratatouille

Each serving 5 C. 105 Cals. (440 J.)

120 g. onions (1 large)	30 g. red or green
480 g. tomatoes	pepper
1 kg. marrow (or ½ kg.	25 ml. olive oil (or
courgettes)	30 g. butter)
120 g. aubergines	clove garlic
	seasoning

> Peel and slice onions and tomatoes. De-seed and slice pepper.

If marrow is used, peel and remove seeds before chopping.

Courgettes and aubergines should be trimmed, washed and sliced with skins left on.

Peel and crush garlic.

Put oil or butter and all vegetables in oven-proof dish, season to taste, cover and bake at 350° F (Mark 3) for 1 hour.

Red Cabbage

Each serving 20 C. 220 Cals. (922 J.)

1 red cabbage (1 kg.)	50 ml. wine vinegar
120 g. cooking apple	50 ml. vegetable
60 g. onion (1 small)	cooking oil
30 g. flour	pinch of nutmeg
15 g. brown sugar	garlic salt and pepper
grated rind 1 orange	

> Remove and discard outer leaves of cabbage and any tough main ribs. Wash and shred remaining leaves.

Heat oil and cook cabbage for 5 minutes with lid on pan.

Peel and chop apple and onion and add to cabbage with garlic salt and just enough water to prevent contents sticking to pan.

Bring to boil and simmer in covered pan

until cabbage is tender but still crisp. (Approximately 20 minutes.)

Drain, reserving liquid.

Make a paste with flour, sugar and vinegar, add reserved liquid gradually and cook in another pan until mixture begins to thicken.

Combine sauce and cabbage, add orange rind, nutmeg and pepper.

Can be reheated, or served cold as a salad.

Basic Pilaff Rice

Each serving 20 C. 200 Cals. (796 J.)

120 g. raw long-grain rice	45 g. butter
60 g. onion (1 small)	pinch of saffron
250 ml. chicken stock (see recipe)	seasoning

> Peel and chop onion and fry in heated butter in large pan until transparent.

Rinse rice in cold water, drain and add to onion. Stir over low heat until the rice starts to take colour.

Heat stock and dissolve saffron in it.

Transfer rice to oven-proof dish, pour on stock, season to taste, cover and bake at 350° F (Mark 3) until rice has absorbed liquid. (15 to 20 minutes.)

Fried Savoury Rice

Each serving 20 C. 120 Cals. (503 J.)

120 g. raw long-grain rice	120 g. mushrooms
60 g. onion (1 small)	120 g. tomatoes
	seasoning

> Peel and chop onions, mushrooms and tomatoes.

Rinse rice in cold water then cook in salted boiling water until just tender. (Approximately 15 minutes.) Drain well.

Heat oil in large pan and fry onion, tomatoes and mushrooms until tender.

Add cooked rice to pan, check for seasoning and fry gently until rice starts to brown.

Spanish Salad

Each serving 10 C. 110 Cals. (461 J.)

120 g. cooked rice	25 ml. olive oil
90 g. tomatoes	25 ml. lemon juice
30 g. green peppers	seasoning
60 g. onions (1 small)	

> Peel and chop onions and tomatoes finely. De-seed and chop peppers.

Mix rice with vegetables.

Beat oil, lemon juice and seasoning together and pour over rice mixture and toss thoroughly.

Creamed Spinach

Each serving Negligible C. 110 Cals. (461 J.)

480 g. fresh spinach (trimmed) or frozen	125 ml. chicken stock or water
1 egg yolk	30 g. butter
	seasoning

> If fresh spinach is used clean well.

Melt butter in large pan, add spinach, stock or water and seasoning. Cook until spinach is soft enough to purée.

Drain and cool then rub through sieve or purée in electric blender. Return to pan.

Beat egg yolk and cream together and mix into the purée.

Reheat but do not boil.

Turnip Purée

Each serving 10 C. 115 Cals. (482 J.)

1 kg. young turnips (peeled and trimmed)	50 ml. single cream seasoning
30 g. butter	

> Cut turnips roughly and cook in a little boiling salted water until tender.

Drain well and rub through sieve or purée in electric blender.

Blend in cream and butter and check seasoning.

Reheat but do not boil.

Vegetable Casserole

Each serving 30 C. 310 Cals. (1299 J.)

360 g. potatoes	50 ml. cooking oil
360 g. young carrots	mixed herbs
360 g. shelled peas	water
180 g. onions (3 small)	seasoning
15 g. butter	

> Scrape and cut carrots into rings. Peel and slice onions and potatoes.

Melt oil and butter in large pan and fry onions until transparent, add carrots and cook for a few minutes.

Transfer to oven-proof dish, add peas, herbs, seasoning and enough water to come half way up contents in dish.

Top with potatoe slices, cover and bake at 350° F (Mark 3) for 1 hour.

Stuffed Marrow Rings

Each serving 5 C. 220 Cals. (920 J.)

1 medium sized marrow	1 teaspoonful chopped parsley
1 medium onion (120 g.)	$\frac{1}{4}$ teaspoon dried thyme
120 g. mushrooms	
120 g. tomatoes	
360 g. lean mince.	seasoning

> Cut marrow into thick even-sized rings, remove skin and seeds and place in lightly greased oven-proof dish.

Peel and chop mushrooms, onions and tomatoes and mix these with the mince, herbs and seasoning.

Fill marrow rings with mixture, cover and bake for 1 hour at 375° F (Mark 4).

Sauces

Each recipe makes four servings except where otherwise stated

Caper Sauce

Each serving 10 C. 105 Cals. (440 J.)

30 g. capers	125 ml. chicken
30 g. butter or margarine	stock (see recipe)
30 g. flour	25 ml. wine vinegar
125 ml. milk	seasoning

> Make a roux with butter and flour. Add milk and stock gradually and stir over low heat until the sauce thickens. Season to taste.

Chop capers finely and stir into sauce. Add vinegar and reheat but do not boil.

Cheese Sauce

Each serving 10 C. 230 Cals. (964 J.)

60 g. grated Cheddar	250 ml. milk
cheese	250 ml. water
45 g. butter or margarine	chopped parsley
45 g. flour	seasoning

> Make a roux with butter and flour.

Add milk and water gradually, bring to boil and stir over low heat until sauce thickens.

Add grated cheese and parsley, season and cook for a further 3 minutes stirring all the time.

Egg Sauce

Each serving 10 C. 215 Cals. (901 J.)

2 hard boiled eggs	250 ml. milk
45 g. flour	250 ml. water
45 g. butter or	chopped parsley
margarine	seasoning

> Make a roux with butter and flour.

Add milk and water gradually, bring to boil and stir over low heat until sauce thickens.

Add chopped hard boiled eggs, parsley and seasoning and cook for a further 3 minutes stirring all the time.

French Dressing

Each 25 ml. serving Negligible C. 60 Cals.
(251 J.)

125 ml. olive oil	15 g. French mustard
75 ml. wine vinegar	garlic salt
7 g. castor sugar	black pepper

> Beat all ingredients together.
   If stored in cool place in covered jar, the dressing can be kept for several days.
   Stir well before use.

Hollandaise Sauce

Each serving Nil C. 300 Cals. (1257 J.)

3 egg yolks	50 ml. boiling water
120 g. butter or	salt
margarine	ground black
1 dessertspoon lemon	pepper
juice	

> Melt butter in double saucepan over hot but not boiling water.

Whisk in lemon juice and egg yolks.
   Cook gently until sauce thickens whisking all the time.
   Add boiling water to make a thin sauce and cook for a further minute.
   Serve hot or cold.

Horseradish Sauce

Each serving Negligible C. 55 Cals. (230 J.)

60 g. fresh horseradish	75 ml. single cream
25 ml. wine vinegar	seasoning

> Grate horseradish. Mix with vinegar and cream.
   Season to taste.

Mayonnaise

Each serving Nil C. 310 Cals. (1299 J.)

1 egg yolk	1 teaspoon wine vinegar
125 ml. olive oil	seasoning

> Beat egg yolk with seasoning and a few drops of the vinegar.
   Beat in oil a drop at a time until mixture thickens.
   The rest of the oil can then be beaten in a teaspoon at a time.
   Add remaining vinegar beating until the mayonnaise is thick and smooth.

Parsley Sauce

Each serving 15 C. 230 Cals. (964 J.)

45 g. flour	chopped parsley
45 g. butter or margarine	seasoning
500 ml. milk	

> Make a roux with butter and flour, add milk gradually, bring to boil and stir over low heat until sauce thickens. Cook for a few moments then remove from heat.

Season, add chopped parsley and serve hot.

Tartare Sauce

Each serving 10 C. 185 Cals. (794 J.)

30 g. flour	1 teaspoon chopped gherkins
30 g. butter or margarine	
250 ml. milk	1 teaspoon chopped parsley
2 egg yolks	
25 ml. single cream	squeeze lemon juice
30 g. chopped capers	seasoning

> Make a roux with butter and flour, add milk gradually, bring to boil and stir over low heat until sauce thickens. Cook gently for a few minutes then remove from heat.

Stir in capers, gherkins and parsley.

Beat yolks well and gradually beat into sauce. Season, add lemon juice and cream.

Before use reheat thoroughly but do not boil.

Egg Custard Sauce

Each serving 10 C. 200 Cals. (838 J.)

500 ml. milk	15 g. granulated sugar
2 eggs	vanilla flavouring

> Heat milk to just below boiling point but do not boil.

Whisk eggs and sugar together and pour milk on gradually. Stir well.

Add a few drops of vanilla essence to taste.

Place egg and milk mixture in top of double saucepan, return to heat and cook gently until the custard starts to thicken stirring all the time. Do not allow to boil or the mixture will curdle.

Serve hot or cold.

Hot Desserts

Each recipe makes four servings except where otherwise stated

Baked Apples

Each serving 20 C. 140 Cals. (478 J.)

4 cooking apples (480 g.)	30 g. butter
40 g. brown sugar	water

> Wash and core apples and, with a sharp knife, make a cut in the skin round middle of each.

Put a quarter of the sugar in the centre of each apple, and top with a quarter of the butter.

Stand apples in oven-proof dish, pour on enough water to come a quarter way up the fruit and bake at 425°F (Mark 6) for $\frac{3}{4}$ to 1 hour.

Baked Stuffed Apples

Each serving 20 C. 110 Cals. (461 J.)

4 cooking apples (480 g.)	30 g. butter
60 g. sultanas	water

> Wash and core apples and, with a sharp knife, make a cut in the skin round middle of each.

Put a quarter of the sultanas in the centre of each apple, and top with the butter evenly divided.

Transfer to oven-proof dish, pour on water to come a quarter way up the fruit and bake at 425°F (Mark 6) for $\frac{3}{4}$ to 1 hour.

Apple Meringue

Each serving 25 C. 270 Cals. (1131 J.)

480 g cooking apples	2 eggs
60 g. butter	juice of 1 lemon
60 g. sugar	

> Peel, core and slice apples. Cook in heavy saucepan with butter, two-thirds of the sugar and lemon juice until very soft. Allow to cool.

Separate eggs, beat yolks into the apple and transfer to lightly greased oven-proof dish.

Whisk whites with remaining sugar until stiff, spoon over apples and bake at 425° F (Mark 6) until meringue is browned.

Apple and Lemon Tart

Each serving 25 C. 260 Cals. (1089 J.)

| shortcrust pastry using 90 g. flour (see recipe) or 120 g. made pastry | 240 g. cooking apples $\frac{1}{2}$ lemon 2 eggs 30 g. sugar |

> Make pastry in usual way and roll out to line a 7-inch flan tin.

Peel and grate apple, grate rind of lemon, squeeze and strain juice.

Mix apple, lemon juice, rind and sugar with beaten eggs.

Pour into flan and bake at 350° F (Mark 3) until set and golden brown. (Approximately 30 minutes.)

Apple Pie

Each serving 25 C. 195 Cals. (817 J.)

| shortcrust pastry using 60 g. flour (see recipe) or 80 g. made pastry 450 g. cooking apples (peeled and cored) | 45 g. sugar cinnamon a little beaten egg |

> Slice apples and place in pie dish. Sprinkle with sugar and cinnamon.

Make pastry in usual way, roll out and cover pie dish, brush with beaten egg and bake at 350° F (Mark 3) for 30 minutes.

Bread and Butter Pudding

Each serving 25 C. 320 Cals. (1341 J.)

60 g. sliced bread	125 ml. water
60 g. butter	30 g. currants
2 eggs	30 g. sugar
375 ml. milk	

> Butter bread, cut into strips and lay on base of oven-proof dish.

Wash currants and sprinkle them on the bread and butter.

Beat together eggs, milk, water and sugar and pour over ingredients in dish.

Bake at 325° F (Mark 2) until set. (Approximately $\frac{3}{4}$ hour.)

Castle Puddings

8 puddings. Each 20 C. 180 Cals. (754 J.)

150 g. self-raising flour	2 eggs
60 g. butter or margarine	juice and rind of 1 lemon
60 g. sugar	water to mix

> Cream together sugar and butter until light and creamy.

Beat eggs and whisk a little at a time into the butter and sugar.

Beat in grated lemon rind and juice.

Fold in flour. (If mixture is too thick to form a dropping consistency, add a little water).

Pour into 8 greased castle pudding moulds.

Bake at 350° F (Mark 3) for 20 minutes.

Baked Custard

Each serving 15 C. 180 Cals. (754 J.)

500 ml. milk	30 g. sugar
3 eggs	vanilla flavouring

> Beat eggs and sugar together.

Heat, but do not boil, milk and add gradually to beaten eggs. Stir in vanilla.

Pour into 4 individual dishes and place in baking tray containing enough water to come quarter way up the dishes.

Bake at 300° F (Mark 1) until set. (Approximately ¾ to 1 hour.)

Lemon Meringue Pudding

Each serving 25 C. 225 Cals. (943 J.)

60 g. bread (without crusts)	2 eggs
500 ml. milk	45 g. sugar
	1 lemon

> Grate rind from lemon and squeeze and strain juice. Add to milk and soak bread in this liquid for half an hour.

Add two-thirds of the sugar, put in saucepan and bring to boil.

Remove from heat and allow to cool.

Separate eggs, beat yolks a little at a time into the mixture.

Transfer to lightly greased oven-proof dish and bake at 350° F (Mark 3) until set. (Approximately 20 minutes.)

Whisk egg whites with remaining sugar until stiff, spoon over pudding, return to oven and bake until meringue top is crisp and brown.

Lemon Pancakes

10 pancakes. Each 10 C. 110 Cals. (461 J.)

120 g. plain flour	30 g. castor sugar
2 eggs	1 lemon
125 ml. milk	oil for cooking
125 ml. water	pinch of salt

> Make batter in usual way. (For method see Yorkshire pudding recipe.)

Stand in cool place for at least an hour before use.

Grease base of omelette pan with a little oil, heat well and pour in a tenth of the mixture.

Cook for about 2 minutes then turn and cook other side for a further minute.

Roll pancakes, sprinkle lightly with the sugar and serve with lemon slices.

Lemon Rice Meringue

Each serving 25 C. 240 Cals. (1006 J.)

37 g. rice (raw)	30 g. butter
250 ml. milk	juice and rind of 1
2 eggs	lemon
60 g. sugar	

> Cook rice in milk, water and butter until tender stirring from time to time. (Approximately 15 to 20 minutes.) Allow to cool.

Separate eggs, beat yolks with half the sugar and add to rice.

Stir in lemon juice and rind and pour mixture into oven-proof dish.

Beat egg whites until stiff, fold in remaining sugar and spoon over rice.

Bake at 275° F (Mark ½) until meringue is set. (Approximately 1 hour.)

Orange Pudding

Each serving 25 C. 240 Cals. (1006 J.)

30 g. flour	2 medium-sized
30 g. margarine	oranges
250 ml. milk	63 ml. fresh orange
45 g. sugar	juice
2 eggs	

> Make a roux with margarine and flour, gradually add milk and stir over low heat until the sauce thickens. Remove from heat and allow to cool.

Separate eggs, add yolks, orange juice and two thirds of the sugar to the sauce.

Beat well.

Peel and divide orange into segments removing pips and pith.

Add most of the segments to the sauce reserving a few for decoration.

Pour mixture into lightly greased oven-proof dish and bake at 350° F (Mark 3) until set. (Approximately 20 to 30 minutes.)

Whisk egg whites with remaining sugar until stiff, spoon over the pudding and decorate with remaining orange segments.

Return to oven, lower heat to 300° F (Mark 1) and bake until meringue is crisp and lightly browned. (Approximately 20 minutes.)

Rice Pudding (or Semolina Pudding)

Each serving 20 C. 180 Cals. (754 J.)

45 g. rice (raw) or	30 g. butter
semolina	45 g. sugar
250 ml. milk	grated nutmeg
250 ml. water	

> Wash rice and put with milk, water, butter and sugar in pie dish.

Sprinkle with grated nutmeg and bake at 350° F (Mark 4) for 2 hours.

Rhubarb and Orange Compote

Each serving 15 C. 70 Cals. (293 J.)

480 g. fresh rhubarb	45 g. brown sugar
2 oranges (120 g.)	

> Wash rhubarb and cut into small pieces.
Peel oranges, remove pith and cut into thin rings.
Put rhubarb, oranges and sugar in oven-proof dish.
Cover and bake at 350° F (Mark 3) for 45 minutes.

Rum Omelette

Each serving 15 C. 280 Cals. (1173 J.)

6 eggs
60 g. castor sugar
100 ml. rum

15 g. butter
vanilla flavouring

> Separate eggs and beat whites until stiff.
Beat together yolks and sugar until lemon coloured, and add vanilla.
Fold in egg whites.
Using 1 large or 2 small heavy frying pans, heat butter, make omelette/s in usual way and fold.
Just before serving, warm a spoon, set rum alight in this and pour still flaming over the omelette/s.

Jamaican Bananas

Each serving 20 C. 80 Cals. (335 J.)

4 bananas
100 ml. unsweetened
orange juice
grated rind of
1 orange

45 g. brown sugar
pinch cinnamon
pinch of nutmeg
dessertspoon rum
(if liked)

> Peel bananas and split them lengthwise.
Place in oven-proof dish and sprinkle with the grated orange rind, brown sugar and spices.
Pour orange juice and rum over them and bake at 375° F (Mark 4) for about 15 minutes. Serve hot.

Rich Semolina Pudding

Each serving 20 C. 210 Cals. (880 J.)

45 g. semolina
250 ml. milk
250 ml. water

30 g. butter
45 g. sugar
1 egg

> Wash semolina.
Separate egg and beat yolk into milk and water. Add semolina, sugar and butter.
Beat egg white until stiff and fold into mixture.
Transfer to pie dish and bake at 050° F (Mark 4) for 1 hour.

Cold Desserts

Each recipe makes four servings except where otherwise stated

Apple Custard

Each serving 25 C. 115 Cals. (482 J.)

360 g. cooking apples
45 g. sugar
175 ml. milk
10 g. custard powder
25 ml. lemon juice
1 egg white
15 g. gelatine

> Peel and core apples and put in a saucepan with a very little water and two-thirds of the sugar. Cook until soft and pulpy. Leave to cool then put through a sieve or purée in electric blender.

Make custard with the powder and milk according to maker's instructions. Allow to cool.

Dissolve gelatine in a little boiling water, add lemon and stir into apple purée.

Fold apple mixture into the custard.

Whisk egg white stiffly and fold in.

Transfer to serving dish and leave in cool place to set.

Apple Snow

Each serving 25 C. 100 Cals. (419 J.)

480 g. dessert apples
45 g. sugar
2 egg whites
juice of half lemon
50 ml. water

> Peel, core and dice apples and cook in water and sugar until soft.

Allow to cool then purée in electric blender or rub through sieve. Stir in lemon juice.

Whisk egg whites very stiffly and fold into apple.

Serve chilled in individual dishes.

Banana Fool

Each serving 15 C. 340 Cals. (1425 J.)

120 g. banana (peeled)
250 ml. double cream
30 g. castor sugar
squeeze lemon juice

> Sieve bananas or purée in electric blender.
Mix in lemon juice.
  Whisk cream with sugar and fold in.
  Transfer to serving dish and chill before use.

Blackberry Mousse

Each serving 10 C. 180 Cals. (754 J.)

240 g. blackberries	7½ g. gelatine
30 g. castor sugar	100 ml. double cream
squeeze lemon juice	whites 2 eggs

> Wash blackberries and place in saucepan
with sugar and lemon juice.
  Simmer gently over low heat for 10 minutes.
Strain off juice and rub fruit through a sieve.
  Dissolve gelatine in juice, combine with fruit
purée and leave in cool place to thicken.
  Whisk cream and fold into fruit.
  Whisk egg whites stiffly and fold into
mixture.
  Transfer to serving dish and chill before use.

Blackcurrant Cream

Each serving 5 C. 305 Cals. (1278 J.)

25 ml. concentrated blackcurrant juice	
250 ml. double cream	squeeze lemon juice

> Mix together lemon and blackcurrant juice.
  Whisk cream lighly and fold into fruit juices.
  Serve well chilled in individual glasses.

Brandy Mousse

Each serving 10 C. 420 Cals. (1760 J.)

6 eggs	40 g. sugar
200 ml. double cream	50 ml. brandy

> Separate eggs and whisk yolks and sugar
together until light, creamy and thick.
  Whisk and fold in cream. Stir in brandy.
  Whisk egg white very stiffly and fold into
mixture.
  Serve chilled in individual glasses.

Chocolate Mousse

Each serving 15 C. 450 Cals. (1886 J.)

120 g. plain chocolate	45 g. butter
4 eggs	100 ml. double cream

> Break chocolate into small pieces and put, with butter, in a bowl over a pan of hot water. Beat until melted and smooth. Remove from heat and allow to cool.

Separate eggs, whisk yolks and beat gradually into chocolate mixture.

Whisk whites stiffly and fold into mixture.

Serve chilled in individual glasses decorated with whipped cream.

Chocolate and Orange Mousse

Each serving 30 C. 440 Cals. (1844 J.)

180 g. plain chocolate	7½ g. butter
25 ml. fresh orange juice	3 large eggs
1 level teaspoon grated orange rind	100 ml. double cream

> Melt chocolate in a basin over hot water and beat until smooth.

Add butter and orange rind, beat well and remove from heat.

Separate eggs and beat in yolks one at a time. Stir in orange juice.

Whisk egg whites stiffly and fold into mixture.

Transfer to serving dish and leave in cool place to set.

Decorate with whipped cream.

Coffee Jelly

Each serving 15 C. 60 Cals. (251 J.)

500 ml. strong black coffee	30 g. gelatine
60 g. sugar	vanilla essence

> Heat a quarter of the coffee and dissolve gelatine and sugar in this.

Add remaining coffee and a few drops of vanilla essence.

Pour into a mould and leave in cold place to set.

Floating Islands

Each serving 20 C. 225 Cals. (943 J.)

500 ml. milk	30 g. gelatine
4 eggs	vanilla essence
60 g. sugar	1 teaspoon grated nutmeg

> Separate eggs and beat whites with half the sugar until stiff.

Heat milk and nutmeg in large pan and add beaten whites a spoonful at a time. Cook each meringue for about 3 minutes turning them at least once. Remove from milk and set aside. Take milk off heat.

Using a little of the hot milk, dissolve gelatine. Set aside.

Whisk egg yolks with remaining sugar and beat gradually into cooled milk. Return to low heat and cook for a few minutes stirring all the time. Do not boil.

Remove from heat, stir in dissolved gelatine, transfer to serving dish and top with meringues.

Leave in cool place to set.

Fruit Flan

6 slices. Each 25 C. 130 Cals. (545 J.)

60 g. self-raising flour	120 g. orange segments
60 g. castor sugar	120 g. dessert apples
2 eggs	(thinly sliced)
60 g. banana	5 g. arrowroot
(thinly sliced)	125 ml. water

> Whisk together eggs and sugar until light and creamy.

Sift and fold in flour using metal spoon.

Pour mixture into greased 8-inch flan tin and bake at 425° F (Mark 6) for 10 minutes. Turn out and allow to cool.

Arrange prepared fruit in flan.

Make a paste with arrowroot and a little of the water. Bring remaining water to boil and stir gradually into the arrowroot.

Return to pan and cook until mixture thickens. Cool slightly and pour over fruit in flan.

Leave in cool place to set.

Fresh Fruit Salad

Each serving 15 C. 60 Cals. (251 J.)

2 grapefruits	120 g. orange (peeled)
120 g. dessert apple	120 g. banana (peeled)
(peeled and cored)	2 black grapes

> Wash and cut grapefruit into halves. Scoop out flesh and cut this into small pieces, removing pith.

Divide orange into segments, removing pith. Dice apple finely and slice banana.

Mix all the fruit together and put a quarter into each grapefruit skin. Decorate with halved and de-seeded grapes.

Honeycomb Mould

Each serving 15 C. 150 Cals. (628 J.)

2 eggs	15 g. gelatine
500 ml. milk	2 teaspoons vanilla essence
30 g. sugar	2 tablespoons hot water

> Separate eggs and beat yolks with milk, sugar and vanilla essence.

Transfer to top of double saucepan and cook on low heat but do not boil. When mixture starts to thicken, remove from heat.

Dissolve gelatine in hot water and stir in. Allow to cool.

Whisk egg whites stiffly and fold into mixture.

Pour in serving dish or mould and chill before use.

Lemon Soufflé

Each serving 15 C. 160 Cals. (670 J.)

2 eggs	60 g. sugar
2 lemons	30 g. gelatine
125 ml. single cream	125 ml. water

> Wash and dry lemons, grate rind and squeeze and strain juice.

Put milk and sugar in a saucepan and bring to boil. Remove from heat and allow to cool.

Separate eggs, beat yolks and whisk these into the milk.

Return to heat and cook gently until mixture thickens, but do not boil. Remove from heat.

Melt gelatine in the water, allow to cool then blend into the egg mixture.

Stir in cream, lemon juice and rind.

Whisk egg whites until very stiff and fold in.

Transfer to souffle dish and leave in cool place to set.

Orange Whip

Each serving 15 C. 60 Cals. (251 J.)

250 ml. fresh orange juice	1 egg white
35 g. sugar	250 ml. water
30 g. gelatine	

> Dissolve gelatine and sugar in a little heated water. Add remaining water and orange juice. Leave in cool place until it starts to set.

Add egg white and whisk thoroughly until jelly is very frothy.

Transfer to serving dish and leave to set. Serve chilled.

Peach Trifle

Each serving 15 C. 450 Cals. (1886 J.)

4 peaches (480 g.)	15 g. sugar
30 g. ground almonds	7 g. gelatine

25 ml. dry sherry   red colouring
300 ml. double cream

> Peel peaches (see Glossary), cut in halves and remove stones.

Poach in a little water until fruit is just tender.

Toast almonds under grill until golden brown, mix with sherry and fill peach centres with mixture.

Dissolve gelatine and sugar in 2 tablespoons hot water. Allow to cool.

Whisk gelatine with half the cream, add colouring and leave to set.

Coat each peach half with the mixture, transfer to serving dish and leave in cool place.

Decorate with remaining cream, whisked stiffly, before serving.

Spiced Pears

Each serving 15 C. 60 Cals. (251 J.)

1 large orange	480 g. dessert pears
(120 g.)	$\frac{1}{4}$ teaspoon ground ginger
1 lemon	

> Squeeze juice from orange and lemon, strain and put in saucepan with two tablespoons water and the ginger.

Peel and core pears, cut in half and add to pan.

Bring to boil and simmer in covered pan for 20 minutes turning fruit from time to time.

Arrange pears in serving dish, pour on liquid and serve chilled.

Raspberry Soufflé

Each serving 20 C. 295 Cals. (398 J.)

480 g. raspberries	60 g. castor sugar
(fresh or frozen	$\frac{1}{2}$-$7\frac{1}{2}$ g. gelatine
without sugar)	125 ml. double cream
3 eggs	

> Cook raspberries very slowly in a saucepan until they are soft and pulpy.

Separate two of the eggs and whisk the yolks with remaining whole egg. Put in a bowl with the sugar over pan of hot water and beat until light and fluffy.

Dissolve gelatine in a little hot water, cool and add to the egg and sugar mixture. Stir in raspberries.

Whisk cream until stiff and fold in.

Whisk remaining two egg whites stiffly and fold into mixture.

Transfer to serving dish and leave in cold place to set.

Semolina Snow

Each serving 20 C. 90 Cals. (377 J.)

60 g. semolina (raw)	rind and juice of 1 lemon
45 g. sugar	500 ml. water

> Blend semolina with enough water to form a smooth paste. Add grated lemon rind and sugar.

Heat remaining water and stir gradually into the semolina paste.

Return to pan, bring to boil and cook until the mixture starts to thicken.

Transfer to a mixing bowl, stir in lemon juice and allow to cool.

Whisk until light and fluffy, transfer to serving dish and chill before use.

Strawberry Blancmange

Each serving 30 C. 165 Cals. (691 J.)

45 g. cornflour	500 ml. milk
45 g. sugar	strawberry flavouring

> Make a paste with cornflour and a little of the milk.

Put remaining milk and sugar in a saucepan, bring to boil and gradually stir into cornflour. Return to pan and cook until mixture thickens.

Remove from heat and stir in flavouring.

Pour into mould and leave in cold place to set.

Syllabub

Each serving 15 C. 295 Cals. (1236 J.)

150 ml. double cream 60 g. castor sugar
1 egg white 50 ml. dry sherry

> Whip cream stiffly.

Whip egg white with sugar until stiff, then fold in sherry and cream.

Serve chilled in individual glasses.

Lemon Sponge

Each serving 15 C. 60 Cals. (251 J.)

15 g. gelatine powder 250 ml. water
rind and juice of 60 g. castor sugar
  1 lemon whites of 2 eggs

> Peel rind from lemon thinly, and squeeze juice.

Put juice, rind, gelatine, water and sugar in saucepan over low heat and stir until gelatine has dissolved. Bring to boil, strain and cool.

Whisk egg whites until stiff, add the lemon mixture gradually whisking all the time.

When it starts to thicken, pour into a mould and leave in cool place to set.

Zabaglione

Each serving 10 C. 155 Cals. (649 J.)

3 egg yolks 125 ml. dry sherry
45 g. sugar

> Beat egg yolks and sugar together in large basin. When light and creamy, stir in sherry.

Put basin over a pan of hot water and continue beating until mixture has thickened and risen.

Serve hot or cold in individual glasses.

Orange Surprise

Each serving 20 C. 185 Cals. (759 J.)

4 oranges 100 ml. unsweetened
4 eggs orange juice
45 g. castor sugar 2 tablespoons
  unsweetened lemon
  juice

> Cut tops off oranges and, with a sharp knife, scrape out pulp. Remove pips and skin from segments.

Separate eggs and beat yolks with orange and lemon juice and sugar.

Put in double saucepan over hot water and cook until mixture starts to thicken stirring all the time.

Remove from heat and allow to cool, then mix with the orange pulp.

Beat egg whites until stiff, fold into mixture and spoon back into the oranges.

Chill and serve.

Party Recipes

Each recipe makes four servings except where otherwise stated

Very rich party sweets cannot be included in a cookery book designed for those who have to consider their food values, but a number of the desserts in the Hot and Cold Dessert sections are suitable for a party.

Starters

Cream of Asparagus Soup

Each serving 5 C. 330 Cals. (1383 J.)

480 g. asparagus (tinned or fresh)	20 g. flour
	30 g. onion (½ small)
1 litre chicken stock (see recipe)	125 ml. double cream
	1 egg yolk
60 g. butter	seasoning

>If asparagus is fresh, trim and boil in stock for 5 minutes.
Tinned asparagus should be drained and liquid discarded.
Set aside a few tips for garnishing.

Peel and chop onion.
Melt butter in large saucepan and fry onion until transparent.
Blend in flour, add stock gradually and stir over low heat until it starts to thicken.
Add asparagus, bring to boil and simmer for 10 minutes.
Remove from heat, cool and rub through sieve or purée in electric blender.
Beat egg yolk and cream together and beat into a little of the purée. Add remaining purée and season to taste.
Reheat but do not allow to boil and serve garnished with reserved asparagus tips.

Dressed Avocado Pears

Each serving Negligible C. 180 Cals. (751 J.)

2 avocado pears	1 dessertspoon chopped fresh mint
100 ml. French dressing (see recipe)	

73

> Cut pears in half and remove stones.
  Chop mint leaves very finely and mix with French dressing.
  Pour 25 ml. dressing into each pear half.

Iced Avocado Pear Soup

Each serving Negligible C. 400 Cals. (1676 J.)

2 large avocado pears (240 g.)	1 teaspoon Worcester sauce
100 ml. plain yoghourt	juice 1 lemon
250 ml. double cream	chopped chives
250 ml. jellied chicken stock (see recipe)	seasoning

> Remove and discard skin and stones of pears and pour lemon juice over flesh immediately to prevent discolouration.
  If a bouillon cube is used, dissolve a level teaspoon of gelatine in the water before pouring it on the cube. Strain stock and cool before use.
  Put avocado flesh yoghourt and stock in electric blender to reduce to consistency of thick cream. Add Worcester sauce and season to taste.
  Whip cream lightly and fold into the soup.
  Chill and serve garnished with chopped chives.

Chicken Liver Paté

Each serving Nil C. 240 Cals. (1006 J.)

240 g. chicken livers	pinch of mixed herbs
75 ml. single cream	seasoning
90 g. butter	

> Mince chicken livers and fry gently in heated butter until the liver is cooked through. (About 8 to 10 minutes.) Allow to cool.
  Mix in cream, herbs and seasoning. Rub through sieve or put through electric blender.
  Transfer to lightly buttered dish and chill before use.

Iced Cucumber and Yoghourt Soup

Each serving 5 C. 100 Cals. (419 J.)

480 g. peeled cucumber	525 ml. plain yoghourt
2 tablespoons finely chopped fresh mint	1 clove garlic
	$\frac{1}{4}$ teaspoon red pepper
	salt

> Slice cucumber paper thin. Crush garlic.
  Mix together yoghourt, cucumber, garlic, red pepper and half the mint. Season to taste.
  Put in individual dishes and chill.
  Just before serving, garnish with remaining mint.

Egg and Horseradish Starter

Each serving Negligible C. 240 Cals. (1006 J.)

4 hardboiled eggs	150 ml. tinned consommé
50 ml. horseradish sauce	10 g. curry powder
125 ml. double cream	salt

> Chill consomme.

Shell eggs and chop finely, add horseradish sauce, curry powder, consommé and seasoning. Mix well together.

Whip cream lightly and fold into mixture.

Serve chilled in individual dishes.

Egg Mimosa

Each serving Negligible C. 100 Cals.(419 J.)

4 hard boiled eggs	seasoning
120 g. peeled shrimps	lettuce leaves
25 ml. salad cream	

> Shell eggs and cut in half lengthwise.

Scoop out yolks and rub through a sieve.

Reserve a little of the sieved yolk for garnishing, and blend the rest with salad cream. Mix in shrimps and spoon the mixture into the egg whites.

Garnish with reserved yolk and serve on bed of lettuce.

Egg and Prawn Jelly

Each serving Nil C. 155 Cals. (649 J.)

1 large tin consommé	60 g. peeled prawns
1 egg	seasoning
½ large cucumber	

> Cook eggs in boiling water for exactly 5 minutes. Plunge in cold water and shell carefully.

Peel and chop half the cucumber very finely and slice the rest thinly.

Stand tin of consommé in hot water until the soup liquifies.

Arrange eggs in soufflé dish points towards centre with prawns and chopped cucumber between them. Season and pour on enough consommé to cover. Allow to set.

Put layer of sliced cucumber on top, pour on remaining consommé and chill.

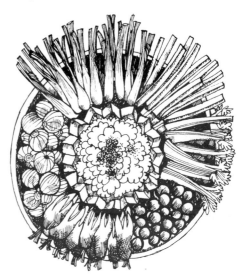

Egg and Prawn Mould

Each serving Negligible C. 230 Cals. (964 J.)

60 g. peeled prawns	2 teaspoons curry
4 hard boiled eggs	powder (optional)
100 ml. double cream	1 teaspoon anchovy
60 g. finely diced	essence
cucumber	2 teaspoons Worcester
175 ml. made aspic	sauce
jelly	seasoning
	water cress

> Shell eggs and chop roughly.

Make aspic according to instructions on packet and allow to cool but not to set. Blend in curry powder, anchovy essence, Worcester sauce and seasoning and add to eggs.

Rub through sieve or blend in electric mixer.

Mix in prawns and diced cucumber.

Whip cream lightly and fold in.

Leave to set in ring mould in refrigerator.

Turn out and serve garnished with water cress.

Gazpacho

Each serving 15 C. 150 Cals. (628 J.)

630 g. tomatoes	300 ml. chicken stock
270 g. cucumber	(see recipe)
240 g. Spanish onions	1 small clove garlic
210 g. green peppers	$7\frac{1}{2}$ g. castor sugar
30 ml. olive oil	(1 level teaspoon)
20 ml. wine vinegar	salt and black pepper

> Chill chicken stock.

Skin and chop roughly tomatoes and cucumber, and de-seed and chop green peppers. Peel and crush garlic. Set aside a quarter for garnishing.

Put rest of prepared vegetables in electric blender, add oil, vinegar, sugar and seasoning and reduce to a smooth purée.

Transfer to large bowl, add chicken stock, check seasoning and chill for at least three hours before use.

Serve in individual dishes, accompanied by reserved vegetables chopped finely and sprinkled on top.

Melon with Brandy

Each serving Negligible C. 95 Cals. (398 J.)

1 medium-sized honeydew melon	100 ml. brandy

> Choose a really ripe melon and cut it into quarters.

With a sharp knife, remove seeds and slice flesh away from skin.

Cut flesh into cubes, place in dish with well-fitting lid, pour on brandy, cover and chill for 2 hours.

Remove from refrigerator, replace flesh on skin, pour brandy and juices from dish evenly on the melon quarters and serve immediately.

Melon and Prawn Cocktail

Each serving Negligible C. 130 Cals. (545 J.)

1 small melon	paprika
150 g. shelled prawns	chopped parsley
125 ml. sour cream	

> With sharp knife remove skin and seeds from melon and dice flesh finely.

Mix sour cream, diced melon and prawns together, season with paprika. Chill and serve garnished with chopped parsley.

Mussel Soup

Each serving Negligible C. 170 Cals. (712 J.)

480 g. mussels	50 ml. olive oil
480 g. peeled tomatoes	1 litre water
2 teaspoons garlic salt	pepper

> Shell mussels, place flesh in the water and leave for at least 1 hour.

Heat oil in large saucepan, add tomatoes and garlic salt and cook gently for 10 minutes.

Rub through sieve or purée in an electric blender, and return to pan.

Strain the liquid from mussels and add this to the purée.

Cook for 20 minutes.

Add mussels and cook for a further 3 minutes.

Serve hot.

Prawn Cocktail

Each serving 5 C. 415 Cals. (1739 J.)

300 g. shelled prawns	50 ml. tomato purée
125 ml. mayonnaise	seasoning
(see recipe)	lettuce
15 g. onion (1 button)	

> Peel and chop onion very finely and mix with mayonnaise, tomato purée and seasoning

Line 4 individual glasses with washed and shredded lettuce leaves and put a quarter of the prawns in each.

Pour on mayonnaise mixture and serve chilled.

Potted Shrimps

Each serving Nil. C. 340 Cals. (1425 J.)

360 g. shrimps (peeled)	pinch of cayenne
120 g. butter	pepper
pinch of ground mace	pinch of nutmeg

> Reserve 20 g. of the butter for clarifying, and melt the rest in frying pan.

Add shrimps, pepper, mace and nutmeg to the pan and cook gently until shrimps are thoroughly heated through, but do not allow to boil.

Divide mixture into four individual serving dishes.

When cold, cover with clarified butter (see glossary) and store in refrigerator until ready to serve.

Taramasalata

Each serving 5 C. 240 Cals. (1006 J.)

180 g. smoked cod's roe	75 ml. olive oil
15 g. bread (without crusts)	25 ml. lemon juice
25 ml. milk	1 small clove garlic
	chopped parsley
	black pepper

> Remove and discard skin and put roe in mixing bowl.

Peel and crush garlic and add to roe.

Pour milk over bread and allow to stand for a few minutes, then squeeze out the milk and add bread to the roe. Mix thoroughly with wooden spoon.

Beat in lemon juice and oil alternately a little at a time.

Season with pepper and chill for at least 2 hours before use.

Serve garnished with parsley.

Main Courses

Beef Carbonnade

Each serving 10 C. 420 Cals. (1760 J.)

720 g. stewing beef (trimmed)	30 g. flour
180 g. onions (3 small)	500 ml. brown ale
45 g. butter	50 ml. tomato purée
	seasoning

> Peel and slice onion and fry in half the butter until transparent.

Cut meat into cubes and brown lightly in remaining butter.

Transfer meat to ovenproof dish leaving juices in the pan.

Make a roux with the juices and flour, blend in tomato purée, add ale gradually and stir over low heat until the sauce begins to thicken.

Add onions and sauce to the meat, season to taste and bake in covered dish at 325° F (Mark 2) for 2 hours.

Fillet of Beef Diane

Each serving Negligible C. 430 Cals. (1802 J.)

4 fillet steaks (480 g. trimmed)	tablespoon chopped parsley
120 g. butter	50 ml. Worcester sauce
15 g. flour	seasoning

> Beat steaks until paper thin and toss in seasoned flour.

Melt butter in large frying pan, add Worcester Sauce and simmer for 3 minutes.

Raise heat under pan and fry steaks for 1 minute. Turn, scatter parsley in pan and cook steaks for a further minute.

Serve immediately with cooking juices.

Beef Strogonoff

Each serving 5 C. 610 Cals. (2556 J.)

720 g. rump steak	60 g. onions (1 small)
30 g. flour	240 ml. sour cream
60 g. butter	juice 1 lemon
240 g. mushrooms	seasoning

> Cut steak into strips approximately $\frac{1}{4}$ inch by 2 inches, and toss in seasoned flour.

Melt half the butter and fry steak for 5 minutes. Transfer to serving dish and keep hot.

Peel and chop onion. Peel and slice mushrooms.

Fry onions and mushrooms in remaining butter until onions are lightly browned. Add to meat and season to taste.

Pour sour cream into pan and warm but do not boil. Stir into meat mixture. Serve immediately.

Chicken with Cream

Each serving 10 C. 700 Cals. (2934 J.)

1½ kg. chicken pieces	100 ml. chicken stock
100 ml. dry white wine	(see recipe)
100 ml. single cream	25 ml. cooking oil
30 g. butter	mixed herbs
60 g. flour	seasoning
120 g. onion (1 large)	

> Remove skin from chicken. Peel and slice onion.

Melt butter and oil in large saucepan and fry chicken and onion until both are lightly browned. Add seasoning and herbs.

Cover pan and cook slowly until chicken leaves the bone easily. (Approximately 20 minutes.)

Remove chicken and onion from the pan and set aside.

Make a roux with the flour and fat in the pan, add wine and stock gradually and stir over low heat until the sauce thickens.

Return chicken and onion to pan and cook gently for a further 10 minutes in the sauce.

Transfer chicken and onion to heated serving dish, stir cream into sauce and pour over chicken.

Devilled Chicken

Each serving Negligible C. 400 Cals. (1676 J.)

4 chicken legs (1 kg.)	1 teaspoon French
15 g. curry paste	mustard

5 g. red currant jelly	salt
50 ml. double cream	

> Mix together curry paste, red currant jelly, mustard and seasoning, spread half of this paste on one side of chicken joints and place them in an ovenproof dish that will fit under the grill.

Leave in cool place for at least 2 hours to marinate.

Heat grill and cook chicken for 15 minutes, then turn joints and spread other side with remaining paste. Grill for further 15 minutes or until chicken leaves the bone easily.

Remove chicken joints, stir cream into cooking juices.

Return chicken to dish and spoon on sauce.

Chicken Kiev

Each serving 20 C. 600 Cals. (2514 J.)

4 boned skinned	120 g. butter
chicken breasts	1 tablespoon chopped
(1 kg.)	parsley
1 egg	vegetable oil for frying
120 g. dry breadcrumbs	seasoning

> Soften butter and blend in parsley and seasoning. Chill.

Beat chicken breasts until thin and on each place a quarter of the parsley butter. Fold to enclose the filling and secure with cotton.

Beat egg, dip chicken pieces and coat with breadcrumbs making sure all the crumbs are used.

Heat oil and fry until chicken is cooked through. (8 to 10 minutes.)

Drain and remove cotton before serving.

Chicken with Peppers

Each serving 15 C. 940 Cals. (3938 J.)

1½ kg. chicken pieces	60 g. red peppers
90 g. flour	125 ml. chicken stock
150 g. butter	(see recipe)
120 g. button onions	125 ml. single cream
120 g. button	150 ml. dry white wine
mushrooms	seasoning
60 g. celery (trimmed)	

> Toss chicken pieces in 60g. of flour and fry in 120g. of the butter until lightly browned. Transfer to ovenproof dish with cooking juices.

Peel onions. Wash mushrooms. Slice celery and de-seed and slice peppers. Add these to the chicken and pour on stock and wine. Season to taste.

Cover and cook at 350° F (Mark 3) for 1 hour.

Remove chicken and vegetables from the liquor, set aside and keep hot.

Boil liquor until it has reduced to about 250 ml.

Make a roux with remaining butter and flour, add reduced liquor gradually and stir over low heat until the sauce thickens.

Remove from heat, stir in cream and pour sauce over chicken and vegetables. Serve immediately.

Coq au Vin

Each serving 5 C. 840 Cals. (3520 J.)

900 g. chicken pieces	50 ml. brandy
240 g. streaky bacon	365 ml. dry red wine

45 g. butter	bouquet garni
15 g. flour	½ clove garlic
240 g. button onions	½ teaspoon dried thyme
240 g. button	2 tablespoons chopped
mushrooms	parsley
30 g. spring onions	seasoning
150 ml. chicken stock	
(see recipe)	

> Peel button and spring onions and leave whole. Wipe over mushrooms. Dice bacon. Skin chicken joints. Crush garlic.

Melt 15g. butter in large frying pan, add bacon and cook until bacon fat runs then discard bacon, reserving fat.

Fry button onions until browned, remove from pan and set aside.

Add remaining butter to pan and fry spring onions and mushrooms lightly. Remove and set aside.

Fry chicken joints until brown then transfer to large ovenproof dish.

Warm a spoon, pour brandy into this, set it alight and pour still flaming over chicken. When the flames are out, add bouquet garni, thyme, garlic and button onions to the chicken.

Make a roux with the fat in the pan and flour, add wine and stock gradually and stir over low heat until sauce thickens. Season to taste and pour over chicken.

Cover and bake at 350° F (Mark 3) for 30 minutes.

Remove from oven and add mushrooms and spring onions. Return to oven for a further 15 minutes.

Crab with Sherry and Brandy

Each serving 5 C. 540 Cals. (2263 J.)

480 g. crab meat
120 g. butter
25 ml. olive oil
120 g. onions (1 large)
90 g. leeks (trimmed)
60 g. tomatoes
30 g. soft breadcrumbs
75 ml. dry sherry
75 ml. brandy

75 ml. chicken stock (see recipe)
1 clove garlic
2 tablespoons chopped parsley
cayenne pepper
black pepper
salt

> Heat half the butter and oil in large pan, add peeled garlic and fry until browned. Remove and discard garlic.

Peel and chop onions, leeks and tomatoes.

Fry onions and leeks in the garlic flavoured fat until transparent. Add tomatoes, sherry and brandy and cook for five minutes until mixture has thickened.

Add crab meat, chicken stock, parsley, cayenne pepper, black pepper and salt to taste. Stir over heat for 2 to 3 minutes.

Transfer to ovenproof serving dish.

Heat remaining butter in pan and cook breadcrumbs until lightly browned, sprinkle over the crab meat mixture and bake at 450° F (Mark 7) for 15 minutes.

Duck in Orange Sauce

Each serving 10 C. 980 Cals. (4106 J.)

1 large duck (2 kg.)
60 g. butter
480 g. orange, peeled (4 large)

50 ml. dry sherry
500 ml. water
seasoning

> Simmer giblets in salted water for 1 hour.
Wash duck thoroughly, butter inside and wrap in foil.

Roast at 375° F (Mark 4) for 2 hours.

Grate rind from 1 orange and remove skin and pith from all. Cut into slices.

Strain giblet stock and add orange rind and sherry.

Reserve a few orange slices for garnishing and add rest to the stock. Season, bring to boil and cook until reduced to consistency of thick sauce.

Pour sauce over duck and garnish with orange slices.

Hake in Tomato Sauce

Each serving 15 C. 425 Cals. (1781 J.)

720 g. hake
60 g. onions (1 small)
120 g. tomatoes
480 g. small new potatoes
75 ml. olive oil
4 garlic cloves

2½ teaspoon paprika
1 teaspoon wine vinegar
1 bay leaf
1½ litres water
salt

> Scrape potatoes. Peel and slice onions and tomatoes.

Bring water to boil, add potatoes, bayleaf salt and onions and simmer until potatoes are cooked.

Remove potatoes and onions, set aside and keep hot. Retain water.

Skin and bone fish and cook in the water until tender. (About 10 minutes.) Remove from heat and leave in the liquid.

Heat oil, add peeled garlic cloves and cook until lightly browned.

Remove garlic and discard. Add tomatoes to pan and cook quickly in the oil until mushy. Blend in paprika.

Pour off fish liquid except for 250 ml., discard bay leaf and return potatoes and onions to pan.

Sieve tomato mixture over fish, bring to boil and simmer for 5 minutes.

Add vinegar, transfer to heated dish and serve.

Roast Lamb

Each serving Nil C. 620 Cals. (2598 J.)

1 small leg of lamb (1½ kg.)	mixed herbs
150 ml. vegetable oil	250 ml. dry red wine
50 ml. wine vinegar	seasoning

> Make a marinade with oil, vinegar, herbs and seasoning.

Pour this over the lamb and leave for at least 3 hours. Turn from time to time to ensure the marinade reaches all surfaces.

Put joint into baking dish with the marinade, cover with foil and roast at 375° F/Mark 4 allowing 30 minutes per ½ kilo.

30 minutes before end of cooking time, pour off and discard cooking juices, pour wine over the joint and return to oven. Baste once or twice.

Pour off wine and keep it hot while you carve, then serve with the meat.

Lobster in White Wine

Each serving Nil C. 490 Cals. (2053 J.)

480 g. lobster meat (cooked)	125 ml. single cream
125 ml. dry white wine	3 egg yolks
125 ml. double cream	seasoning

> Pour the double cream into large frying pan and heat to just below boiling point.

Beat single cream with egg yolks, add to the pan and cook until sauce thickens. Do not boil.

Add wine, lobster meat and seasoning and reheat.

Serve immediately.

Moussaka

Each serving 10 C. 390 Cals. (1634 J.)

600 g. lean fresh mince	garlic salt
30 g. grated Cheddar cheese	black pepper
240 g. tomatoes	For sauce:
480 g. aubergines	30 g. flour
180 g. onions (3 small)	30 g. butter
1 green pepper	175 ml. chicken stock (see recipe)
cooking oil	seasoning

> Slice but do not peel aubergines, sprinkle with salt and leave for at least half an hour. Rinse off salt and pat dry on a cloth. Peel and dice onion. Peel and slice tomatoes. De-seed and slice pepper.

Heat oil in large (preferably non-stick) frying pan and fry aubergine slices until golden brown. Set aside.

Fry onions until transparent, add mince and green pepper to pan and cook until meat is lightly browned. Season to taste.

Put half the mince in ovenproof dish, add layer of aubergine slices sprinkled with a little cheese. Add rest of mince, then remaining aubergine slices sprinkled with cheese and top with tomato slices.

Make a roux with butter and flour, add stock gradually and stir on low heat until sauce thickens. Reserve a little of the remaining cheese to sprinkle on top and blend the rest into the sauce. Season to taste and pour sauce over other ingredients in dish.

Bake at 400° F (Mark 5) for 25 to 30 minutes.

Paella

Each serving 25 C. 445 Cals. (1865 J.)

480 g. cooked chicken meat	120 g. tomatoes
120 g. shelled prawns	60 g. onions (1 small)
120 g. mussels (shelled)	1 litre chicken stock (see recipe)
90 g. long-grain rice (raw)	1 clove garlic
150 g. peas (fresh or frozen)	50 ml. olive oil
120 g. green or red peppers	pinch saffron seasoning

> Skin and dice chicken. Peel and slice onion and tomatoes.

De-seed and slice peppers. Peel and crush garlic.

Cook mussels in a little boiling water for 3 minutes. Drain and set aside. Put rice in a sieve and run cold water through it.

Melt oil in large pan and fry chicken, onion and garlic until golden brown.

Add 500 ml. stock, bring to boil and simmer for 15 minutes.

Add tomatoes, rice, remaining stock and saffron. Simmer for a further 5 minutes.

Add prawns, peppers and peas and continue cooking until rice has absorbed the stock but is not dry. Check seasoning. Mix in mussels and serve hot.

Barbecued Pork Chops

Each serving 5 C. 980 Cals. (4106 J.)

4 thick lean pork chops (1 kg.)	juice of 1 lemon
60 g. butter	15 g. mustard powder
180 g. tomatoes	50 ml. Worcester sauce
60 g. celery (trimmed)	1 clove garlic
15 g. brown sugar	mixed herbs
250 ml. dry red wine	seasoning

> Skin tomatoes and purée in electric blender or rub through sieve.

Melt butter in large pan, add chops and brown each side. Transfer to ovenproof dish.

Chop celery finely and mix with wine, tomato purée, lemon juice, brown sugar, mustard, Worcester sauce, crushed garlic, mixed herbs and seasoning.

Pour over chops, cover and bake at 350° F (Mark 3) for 1 hour.

Remove cover and continue cooking for further ½ hour.

Pork Chops in Red Wine

Each serving 5 C. 625 Cals. (2619 J.)

4 pork chops (1 kg.) 50 ml. olive oil
30 g. flour 125 ml. dry red wine
60 g. butter chopped parsley
60 g. onion (1 small) seasoning

> Toss chops in seasoned flour making sure that all the flour is used.

Melt butter and oil in large pan and fry chops until tender.

Drain and transfer to serving dish. Keep hot.

Peel and chop onions finely and fry in fat until lightly browned.

Transfer to serving dish.

Add wine to pan and simmer until reduced by half.

Pour wine over chops and onions and serve garnished with parsley.

Sauté of Pork

Each serving 10 C. 700 Cals. (2934 J.)

720 g. pork spareribs 180 ml. dry red wine
(boned) 180 ml. stock or water
240 g. tomatoes 45 g. butter
120 g. button onions 30 g. flour
120 g. green peppers pinch dried rosemary
60 g. black olives seasoning

> Cut pork into large cubes.

Skin and quarter tomatoes. De-seed and dice peppers.

Peel and slice onions. Cut olives in half and remove stones.

Melt butter in large pan and fry onions until transparent.

Transfer to ovenproof dish.

Toss pork in seasoned flour and brown in remaining butter in pan. Add, with cooking juices, to the onions.

Add tomatoes, pepper, olives and rosemary to the dish and pour on wine and stock.

Cover and cook at 300° F (Mark 1) for $2\frac{1}{2}$ hours.

Salmon Steaks in Foil

Each serving Nil C. 340 Cals. (1425 J.)

4 salmon steaks 1 tablespoon chopped
(about 150 g. each) parsley
30 g. butter juice of 1 lemon
 seasoning

> Cut four pieces of foil large enough to allow a good overlap for sealing, and butter well.

Season steaks and sprinkle with parsley and lemon juice on both sides.

Wrap in the foil and bake at 350° F (Mark 3) for 20 minutes.

Unwrap and serve hot with cooking juices poured over the fish.

Savoury Esau

Each serving 10 C. 325 Cals. (1362 J.)

480 g. lean stewing 60 g. carrots
steak 60 g. celery (trimmed)
25 g. butter 2 bay leaves

30 g. flour   900 ml. stock or water
120 g. onions (1 large)   seasoning

> Peel and slice all vegetables and fry in heated butter until lightly browned. Transfer to ovenproof dish.

Cut meat into four portions, brown in fat remaining in pan and add to vegetables.

Pour on stock, add bay leaves and bouquet garni, season and cook for $1\frac{1}{2}$ hours in covered dish at 350° F (Mark 3).

Remove meat from dish and set aside. Remove and discard bay leaves and bouquet garni.

Add flour to vegetables and rub through a sieve or purée in electric blender.

Cook in saucepan over low heat until purée thickens.

Return meat to dish, pour on vegetable purée and cook for a further 30 minutes.

Sole Bonne Femme

Each serving 5 C. 490 Cals. (2053 J.)

1 kg. sole (8 small fillets)	100 ml. milk
	50 ml. single cream
90 g. butter	250 ml. dry white wine
30 g. onion ($\frac{1}{2}$ small)	25 ml. lemon juice
30 g. flour	chopped parsley
90 g. mushrooms	seasoning

> Roll skinned and boned fillets and place greased ovenproof dish.

Pour on wine and lemon juice. Add parsley and seasoning.

Bake at 350° F (Mark 3) for 20 to 25 minutes.

Meanwhile peel and slice onion and mushrooms and fry in two-thirds of the butter until the onion is transparent. Remove onion and mushrooms from pan, set aside and keep hot.

Make a roux in the pan with remaining butter and flour, add milk gradually and stir over low heat until sauce thickens.

Strain cooking juices from the fish into the sauce, add mushrooms and onion and cook for a further few minutes.

Remove from heat and stir in cream, check for seasoning and pour sauce over fish.

Sole and Lobster Mornay

Each serving 10 C. 600 Cals. (2514 J.)

1 kg. sole	30 g. flour
(8 small fillets)	90 g. butter
120 g. lobster meat	125 ml. milk
250 ml. dry white wine	50 ml. single cream
1 hard boiled egg	lemon juice
60 g. grated Cheddar cheese	seasoning

> Remove skin and bones from sole.

Roll fillets and put in ovenproof dish with wine, lemon juice and a third of the butter.

Cover and bake for 15 minutes at 375° F (Mark 4).

Make a roux with flour and remaining butter, add milk gradually and stir over low heat until sauce thickens. Season to taste.

Dice lobster and add, with cream, to the sauce.

Reheat but do not boil and pour sauce over sole fillets.

Garnish with sliced hard boiled egg, sprinkle with grated cheese and brown under hot grill.

Sole and Prawns in Sauce

Each serving 10 C. 600 Cals. (2514 J.)

1 kg. sole (8 small fillets)	100 ml. double cream
240 g. shelled prawns	250 ml. milk
(fresh or frozen)	juice of 1 lemon
60 g. butter	seasoning
30 g. flour	

> Remove skin and any bones from fillets and roll loosely.

Place in ovenproof dish, pour on lemon juice and season.

Dot with half the butter and pour on 50 ml. of the milk.

Bake at 350° F/Mark 3 for 10 minutes.

Remove from oven and fill each roll with prawns. Return to oven and bake for a further 10 minutes. Remove from dish and keep hot.

Make a roux with remaining butter and flour, gradually add rest of the milk and stir over low heat until sauce thickens. Season to taste. Add fish cooking juices and cook for a further few minutes. Remove from heat and stir in cream.

Return fish rolls to dish and pour on sauce.

Steak in Sherry Sauce

Each serving Negligible C. 525 Cals. (2200 J.)

960 g. sirloin steak	75 ml. dry sherry
60 g. butter	50 ml. single cream
60 g. onions (1 small)	seasoning
240 g. tomatoes	
(fresh or tinned)	

> If fresh tomatoes are used skin and cook in water until very soft.

Melt butter in large frying pan and fry steaks according to taste. Transfer to serving dish and keep hot.

Peel and dice onions, fry until lightly browned then add tomatoes to pan. Cook for 5 minutes and put through sieve. Season to taste. Stir in sherry.

Add cream to sauce and pour over steaks.

Veal in Madeira Sauce

Each serving 5 C. 360 Cals. (1508 J.)

4 veal escallopes	30 g. onions
(480 g.)	(1 button)
90 g. butter	30 g. carrots
30 g. flour	30 g. bacon
250 ml. brown stock	50 ml. Madeira
(see recipe)	seasoning
60 g. mushrooms	

> Make a roux with a third of the butter and all the flour, add stock gradually and stir over low heat until sauce thickens.

Dice bacon. Peel and dice finely mushrooms, onions and carrots and add these to the sauce.

Bring to the boil and simmer for 20 minutes. Remove from heat and rub through sieve or purée in electric blender. Return to pan, add Madeira and keep hot. Season to taste.

Melt remaining butter and fry escallopes until cooked according to taste. Transfer to heated serving dish and pour on sauce.

Veal Cutlets in Cider

Each serving 10 C. 450 Cals. (1886 J.)

4 veal cutlets (720 g.)	60 g. grated Cheddar
60 g. butter	cheese
120 g. mushrooms	100 ml. dry cider
120 g. onions (1 large)	pinch of dried thyme
60 g. soft breadcrumbs	seasoning

> Heat butter and fry cutlets lightly. Lay on base of ovenproof dish.

Peel and chop onions and mushrooms and fry until onion is transparent. Add breadcrumbs to pan and cook on very low heat for a further minute until crumbs have absorbed all the fat.

Spoon mixture evenly on to the cutlets.

Pour on cider, season and sprinkle with cheese.

Cover and bake at 350° F (Mark 3) for 45 minutes.

Veal Marengo

Each serving Negligible C. 280 Cals. (1173 J.)

720 g. lean veal	$\frac{1}{2}$ teaspoon paprika
250 ml. tomato juice	25 ml. cooking oil
120 g. tomatoes	500 ml. water
90 g. onions (1$\frac{1}{2}$ small)	1 clove garlic
360 g. mushrooms	seasoning

> Cut veal into cubes. Peel and slice tomatoes and mushrooms.

Peel and chop onions finely. Crush garlic.

Heat oil in large pan and fry veal until lightly browned.

Add water, tomato juice, garlic, paprika and seasoning to pan.

Cover, bring to boil and simmer for 45 minutes.

Add tomatoes, onions and mushrooms and simmer for a further 20 minutes.

Veal Garnished

Each serving Negligible C. 605 Cals. (2535 J.)

840 g. veal (trimmed)	120 g. grated Cheddar
90 g. butter	cheese
30 g. mustard powder	black pepper
125 ml. double cream	salt

> Cut veal into 4 thick slices and fry in butter until cooked through.

Mix mustard powder with grated cheese, cream and season to taste.

Put veal slices on shallow baking tray, pour the fat in which they were cooked over them, spread cheese mixture evenly on each slice and brown under hot grill.

Serve immediately.

Veal Olives

Each serving 10 C. 470 Cals. (1969 J.)

4 veal escallopes (480 g.)	360 g. tomatoes
	60 g. onions (1 small)
60 g. streaky bacon (4 rashers)	30 g. soft breadcrumbs
	150 ml. stock or water
1 egg	mixed herbs
90 g. butter	grated rind ½ lemon
20 g. flour	seasoning

> Mix breadcrumbs with herbs, seasoning and lemon rind and bind with beaten egg.

Peel and slice tomatoes and onions.

Beat escallopes until very thin, place a trimmed rasher on each and a quarter of the stuffing. Roll up and tie with cotton thread.

Heat two-thirds of the butter in pan and fry rolls until lightly browned. Transfer to ovenproof dish and add tomatoes.

Fry onions until transparent and transfer to dish.

Make a roux with flour and remaining third of the butter, add stock gradually and stir over low heat until it starts to thicken. Check for seasoning, and pour sauce over veal and vegetables.

Cover and bake at 350° F (Mark 3) for 1 hour.

Remove cotton thread before serving.

Vegetables

Asparagus Polonaise

Each serving 5 C. 240 Cals. (1006 J.)

1440 g. fresh asparagus (or 720 g. tinned)	1 hard boiled egg
	2 tablespoons chopped parsley
90 g. butter	
30 g. soft breadcrumbs	seasoning

> Prepare fresh asparagus and cook in boiling salted water until tender.

If tinned asparagus is used, heat to boiling point.

Drain and transfer asparagus to ovenproof dish and keep hot.

Melt butter and fry crumbs until crisp and brown. Sprinkle over asparagus and garnish with finely chopped egg and parsley.

Cucumber and Yoghourt Salad

Each serving Negligible C. 40 Cals. (168 J.)

240 g. cucumber	1 tablespoon fresh chopped mint
175 ml. plain yoghourt	
	seasoning

> Slice cucumber finely leaving skin on. Sprinkle with half the mint.

Season yoghourt to taste, pour it over the cucumber and sprinkle with remaining mint.

Chill before serving.

Mushrooms in Cream

Each serving Nil C. 375 Cals. (1571 J.)

480 g. mushrooms	30 g. onion ($\frac{1}{2}$ small)
250 ml. double cream	cayenne pepper
60 g. butter	seasoning

> Peel and chop onion and mushrooms. Fry in heated butter until onion is transparent.

Add cream to pan and reheat until thickened. Do not boil.

Season and serve.

Stuffed Mushrooms

Each serving 15 C. 325 Cals. (1362 J.)

480 g. large mushrooms	60 g. butter
120 g. white soft	1 egg
breadcrumbs	60 g. onion (1 small)
60 g. ham	30 g. parmesan cheese
30 ml. double cream	seasoning

> Peel mushrooms and remove stalks. Peel onion and chop finely.

Chop mushroom stalks and fry, with the onion, in 45 g. of the butter until onion is transparent.

Dice ham, mix with the fried onion mixture and add breadcrumbs.

Bind with beaten egg and cream and season to taste.

Fill mushroom caps with the mixture and place them on ovenproof dish greased with remaining butter.

Sprinkle each cap with Parmesan cheese and bake at 375° F (Mark 4) for 20 minutes.

Stuffed Tomatoes

Each serving 5 C. 120 Cals. (503 J.)

480 g. tomatoes	30 g. soft breadcrumbs
(4 large)	30 g. butter
60 g. lean ham	seasoning
30 g. onion ($\frac{1}{2}$ small)	

> Cut tops off tomatoes and scoop out flesh.

Peel onion and dice finely. Chop ham finely.

Melt butter and fry onion until transparent.

Add breadcrumbs, tomato flesh and seasoning and fry for a few minutes.

Fill tomato cases with the mixture, replace tops and bake at 350° F (Mark 3) for 20 to 25 minutes.

Savouries

Date and Bacon Savoury

Each serving (3 dates) 10 C. 225 Cals. (943 J.)

60 g. stoned dates	120 g. streaky bacon
(12 dates)	(12 rashers)
30 g. grated Cheddar cheese	

> Choose bacon that is cut very thin and remove rind.

Fill each date with grated cheese and wrap a rasher round it. Secure with a cocktail stick.

Bake at 425° F (Mark 6) until bacon is crisp (5 to 10 minutes).

Scotch Woodcock

Each serving 10 C. 290 Cals. (1215 J.)

80 g. bread (4 slices
   without crusts)
30 g. anchovy paste
4 eggs

60 g. anchovy fillets
100 ml. single cream
15 g. butter
seasoning

> Toast bread and spread with butter and anchovy paste.

Grease pan and scramble seasoned eggs. Remove from heat and stir in cream. Divide evenly on to the toast.

Top each portion with an anchovy fillet and serve immediately.

Bakery

American Biscuits

8 biscuits. Each 25 C. 160 Cals. (670 J.)

240 g. self-raising flour	100 ml. milk
45 g. margarine or lard	½ teaspoon salt

> Rub fat into sifted flour and salt, and mix to a dough with milk.

Roll out to 1 inch thickness and cut into 8 fingers.

Bake on lightly greased tray at 425° F (Mark 6) for 15 minutes.

Basic Biscuit Recipe

14 biscuits. Each 10 C. 80 Cals. (335 J.)

120 g. flour	1 egg yolk
60 g. butter or margarine	50 ml. milk
60 g. sugar	flavouring to taste

> Rub fat into sifted flour and sugar to consistency of breadcrumbs.

Beat together egg yolk, milk and flavouring. Add to mixture to form a stiff dough and knead until smooth.

Roll out to ¼ inch thickness, cut into 14 biscuits and bake at 350° F (Mark 3) until crisp and brown. (Approximately 10 to 15 minutes.)

Chocolate Swiss Roll

10 slices. Each 20 C. 150 Cals. (628 J.)

90 g. self-raising flour	30 g. cocoa powder
120 g. castor sugar	75 ml. double cream
3 eggs	1 tablespoon hot water

> Put eggs and sugar in bowl over pan of hot (not boiling) water and whisk until light, creamy and stiff enough to form peaks. Remove from heat.

Sift flour and cocoa, fold half into egg and sugar using a metal spoon, then fold in remainder. Stir in hot water.

Pour mixture into medium-sized Swiss roll tin, lined with lightly-buttered greaseproof paper, allowing mixture to flow evenly over base of tin.

Bake on top shelf of oven at 450° F (Mark 7) for 5 to 10 minutes until golden brown.

Cover while still hot with lightly-buttered greaseproof paper and roll. Leave to cool.

When cold unroll and spread with whipped double cream, re-roll and serve.

Chocolate and Walnut Cake

20 slices. Each 20 C. 190 Cals. (796 J.)

100 g. self-raising flour	180 g. butter or margarine
240 g. sugar	100 g. chopped walnuts
6 eggs	180 g. cocoa powder

> Cream together butter and sugar until light and fluffy, then mix in sifted cocoa.
Separate eggs, beat yolks into mixture, add walnuts and fold in sifted flour.

Whisk egg whites until very stiff and fold into mixture.

Lightly grease a large loaf tin and bake at 350° F (Mark 3) for approximately 1½ to 2 hours.

Coffee Party Cake

32 slices. Each 25 C. 200 Cals. (838 J.)

For cake:

270 g. self-raising flour	4 heaped teaspoons
225 g. margarine	instant coffee powder
240 g. sugar	½ teaspoon
4 eggs	vanilla essence

For icing:

300 g. icing sugar	2 heaped teaspoons
150 g. margarine	instant coffee powder
75 ml. milk	½ teaspoon vanilla essence

> *To make cake,* cream together margarine and sugar until light and fluffy. Beat eggs and gradually beat into the mixture.

Fold in sifted flour and divide mixture in half.

Into one half of the mixture stir in vanilla essence, and into the other half, mix in instant coffee powder dissolved in a little water.

Grease lightly two 8-inch sponge tins and cook the coffee and vanilla cakes for 35 minutes at 350° F (Mark 3).

Remove from tins and cool, then cut coffee section in half horizontally.

To make icing, cream together sifted icing sugar and margarine, add milk and divide mixture into thirds. In one third, mix vanilla essence and into remaining two-thirds mix instant coffee powder.

Spread bottom half of coffee cake with half the vanilla icing, put plain cake on top, spread with remaining vanilla icing.

Top with remaining half of coffee cake and decorate with coffee icing.

Cream Puffs

8 puffs. Each 10 C. 190 Cals. (796 J.)

| 120 g. plain flour | 100 ml. double cream |

60 g. margarine	250 ml. water
2 eggs	pinch of salt

> Put margarine, water and salt into saucepan and bring to boil.

Reduce heat, add flour and mix well. Cook on low heat for a few minutes until mixture starts to leave side of pan.

Remove from heat and allow to cool.

Beat in eggs one at a time and continue beating until mixture is smooth and shiny. (This takes approximately 10 minutes.)

Pipe on to greased baking tray to make 8 puffs.

Bake at 450° F (Mark 7) for 10 minutes, then reduce heat to 375°F (Mark 4) for a further 20 minutes.

When cold, cut off tops of puffs and fill centres with whipped cream.

Date Scones

12 scones. Each 20 C. 170 Cals. (712 J.)

240 g. self-raising flour	1 egg
45 g. lard	75 g. dates (stoned)
45 g. margarine	pinch of salt
30 g. sugar	water to mix

> Rub fat into sifted flour and salt. Mix in sugar.

Chop and add dates.

Add beaten egg and a little water to form a stiff dough, and roll out lightly.

Cut into 12 rounds, place on lightly-greased baking tray and bake at 325° F (Mark 2) for 20 minutes.

Date and Walnut Loaf

12 slices. Each 25 C. 145 Cals. (608 J.)

180 g. self-raising flour	60 g. chopped walnuts
30 g. margarine	½ teaspoon
60 g. sugar	bicarbonate of soda
90 g. dates (stoned)	125 ml. boiling water

> Slice dates and place in basin with bicarbonate of soda and boiling water. Stir well to ensure all bicarbonate is dissolved.

Rub margarine into sifted flour and mix in nuts and sugar.

Make well in middle and pour in water and dates.

Mix quickly together and place in small greased loaf tin.

Bake at 375° F (Mark 4) for 45 minutes.

Dundee Cake

15 slices. Each 25 C. 235 Cals. (985 J.)

240 g. self-raising flour	45 g. sultanas
180 g. margarine	60 g. chopped almonds
120 g. sugar	3 eggs
45 g. currants	50 ml. water
45 g. raisins	

> Cream margarine and sugar until light and fluffy, then gradually beat in eggs.

Wash and add dried fruit, and stir in almonds.

Fold in flour and add enough water to make soft dropping consistency.

Bake in lightly-greased 8-inch cake tin at 350° F (Mark 3) for 2 to 2½ hours.

Easter Cakes

20 cakes. Each 10 C. 80 Cals. (335 J.)

150 g. self-raising flour	90 g. butter or margarine
1 egg yolk	30 g. currants
60 g. castor sugar	grated nutmeg or mixed spice

> Cream together butter and sugar and beat in egg yolk.

Fold in flour, spice and currants and stand in cool place for 15 minutes.

Roll out to ¼ inch thickness and cut into 20 fingers.

Place on lightly-greased baking tray and bake at 350° F (Mark 3) for 15 minutes.

Flaky Pastry

8 servings. Each 25 C. 295 Cals. (1236 J.)

240 g. plain flour	125 ml. water
180 g. butter or margarine	1 teaspoon salt

> Sieve together flour and salt.

Divide butter equally into 4.

Cut a quarter of the butter into small pieces and mix with all the flour. Add chilled water to form an elastic dough.

Roll out on lightly floured board to oblong shape.

Cut another quarter of the butter into pieces and dot two-thirds of pastry, fold into envelope by turning up unbuttered third, and remaining third down. Roll out again to oblong.

Repeat process until all butter is used.

Place in refrigerator for at least half-an-hour before use.

French Madelines

12 Madelines. Each 10 C. 90 Cals. (377 J.)

60 g. self-raising flour	60 g. butter or margarine
60 g. sugar	2 eggs

> Melt butter and allow to cool.

Whisk together eggs and sugar until thick and creamy, then fold in half the flour.

Fold in melted butter and remaining flour.

Grease 12 Madeline tins and half-fill them with the mixture.

Bake at 375° F (Mark 4) for 15 minutes.

Gingerbread Biscuits

30 biscuits. Each 15 C. 100 Cals. (419 J.)

180 g. self-raising flour	1 egg
120 g. margarine	1 teaspoon ground ginger
360 g. sugar	

> Cream together butter and sugar then gradually beat in egg.

Fold in flour and ginger and work with hand until a stiff pliable dough is formed.

Divide mixture into 30 balls, place on lightly-greased baking tray and bake at 300° F (Mark 1) for 40 minutes.

Lemon Cream Biscuits

15 biscuits. Each 15 C. 135 Cals. (566 J.)

195 g. plain flour	grated rind
150 g. butter or margarine	and juice
60 g. sugar	of 1 lemon

> Cream together butter and sugar until light and fluffy, then mix in sifted flour, lemon juice and rind.

Stand in cool place for 15 minutes.

Roll out on lightly-floured board and cut into 15 fingers.

Bake at 350° F (Mark 3) for 15 minutes.

Hot Cross Buns

12 buns. Each 20 C. 135 Cals. (566 J.)

240 g. plain flour	125 ml. water
30 g. sugar	30 g. currants
15 g. yeast	1 egg

60 g. margarine	1 teaspoon mixed spice
125 ml. milk	1 teaspoon salt

> Cream yeast with a little of the sugar until liquid.

Rub together sifted flour, remaining sugar, currants, mixed spice and margarine in warmed bowl.

Heat milk until lukewarm and beat in egg, reserving a little of the egg to use as a glaze. Add to yeast and stir into flour mixture to form a soft dough.

Knead well and leave in warm place to rise to double its size.

Knead again and divide into 12 buns. Place on greased baking tray and leave to rise to twice their size.

Mark with cross using a warmed knife, brush with reserved egg and bake at 425° F (Mark 6) for approximately 25 minutes.

Lemon Queen Cakes

18 cakes. Each 10 C. 110 Cals. (461 J.)

120 g. self-raising flour	2 eggs
120 g. butter or margarine	juice and rind
120 g. castor sugar	of 1 lemon

> Wash lemon, grate rind and squeeze and strain juice.

Cream together sugar and fat until very light and fluffy, then stir in lemon rind.

Beat together eggs and lemon juice and gradually beat into butter and sugar mixture.

Fold in flour and spoon into 18 bun cases.

Bake at 400° F (Mark 5) for 15 minutes.

Malt Loaf

15 slices. Each 20 C. 80 Cals. (335 J.)

240 g. self-raising flour   1 teaspoon
25 ml. malt   bicarbonate of soda
25 ml. golden syrup   water to mix
60 g. dates (stoned)   pinch of salt

> Heat malt and golden syrup in saucepan.
Remove from heat and mix into flour.
    Add bicarbonate of soda, salt and chopped
dates.
    Mix thoroughly then add enough water to
form a stiff dough.
    Line a bread tin with lightly-oiled grease-
proof paper and bake loaf in this at 350° F
(Mark 3) until rich brown. (Approximately
50 minutes.)

Oatcakes

17 oatcakes. Each 10 C. 70 Cals. (293 J.)

240 g. oatmeal   pinch of
30 g. dripping   bicarbonate of soda
½ teaspoon salt   boiling water

> Rub together oatmeal, salt, bicarbonate of
soda and dripping to consistency of
breadcrumbs. Add enough boiling water to
form a soft elastic dough.
    Roll out on lightly-floured board and cut
into 17 equal sized cakes.
    Place on lightly-greased griddle and cook on
one side only.

Turn, transfer to baking tray and bake in
oven at 425° F (Mark 6) until crisp.
(Approximately 5 minutes.)

Plain Buns

20 buns. Each 10 C. 95 Cals. (398 J.)

240 g. self-raising flour   1 egg
90 g. sugar   2 teaspoons
120 g. butter   vanilla essence
   or margarine   water to mix

> Rub fat into sifted flour and sugar to
consistency of breadcrumbs.
    Beat together eggs and vanilla and stir into
flour mixture.
    Add enough water to form soft dropping
consistency, and mix well.
    Divide mixture between 20 bun cases and
bake at 350° F (Mark 3) for 15 to 20 minutes.

Rasberry and Apple Meringue Tarts

15 tarts. Each 15 C. 90 Cals. (377 J.)

shortcrust pastry using 150 g. flour
    (or 160 g. made pastry)
120 g. fresh or unsweetened frozen raspberries
120 g. cooking apple
60 g. sugar
1 egg

> Roll out pastry and cut into 15 rounds.

Line patty tins, prick bases and bake for 20 minutes at 375° F (Mark 4).

Peel, core and slice apple and cook with raspberries and half the sugar for 5 minutes. Cool and beat in egg yolk.

Divide mixture between pastry cases.

Whisk egg white with remaining sugar until stiff. Spread evenly on the tarts and return to oven for 5 to 10 minutes until meringue is lightly browned.

Rich Fruit Cake

30 slices. Each 25 C. 185 Cals. (775 J.)

300 g. self-raising flour	½ teaspoon
240 g. margarine	ground nutmeg
180 g. sugar	½ teaspoon cinnamon
4 eggs	½ teaspoon salt
120 g. sultanas	1 teaspoon
120 g. currants	gravy browning
120 g. raisins	30 g. chopped almonds
120 g. glace cherries	30 g. chopped walnuts
120 g. mixed peel	25 ml. black treacle
1 level teaspoon	50 ml. rum or brandy
mixed spices	

> Sieve together flour, mixed spices, nutmeg, cinnamon, salt and add gravy browning.

Cream margarine and sugar until light and fluffy.

Beat eggs and gradually beat them into margarine and sugar, then add melted treacle mixed with rum.

Fold in flour, add dried fruit, nuts, cherries and peel and mix well.

Line 8-inch cake tin with lightly-oiled greaseproof paper and bake cake in this at 325° F (Mark 2) for 1 hour, then reduce heat to 275° F (Mark ½) for a further 2 to 3 hours.

Rock Cakes

15 cakes. Each 20 C. 150 Cals. (628 J.)

240 g. self-raising flour	1 egg
120 g. margarine	60 g. currants
90 g. castor sugar	50 ml. water

> Rub margarine into sifted sugar and flour to consistency of breadcrumbs.

Mix in washed currants.

Beat egg with water and add to mixture to form a stiff, sticky dough.

Divide into 15 cakes and bake on greased baking tray at 425° F (Mark 6) for 12 to 15 minutes.

Saffron Dough Cake

12 slices. Each 20 C. 120 Cals. (503 J.)

240 g. plain flour	50 ml. water
30 g. butter	75 g. currants
or margarine	8 grains
15 g. yeast	saffron strands
30 g. sugar	¼ teaspoon
1 egg	grated nutmeg
50 ml. milk	pinch salt

> Infuse saffron strands in a little boiling water and leave for at least an hour.

Rub fat into sieved flour and salt. Add currants and nutmeg.

Cream together yeast and sugar until liquid.

Heat milk and water until lukewarm, beat in egg and add to sugar and yeast.

Strain saffron, discard strands and add fluid to other liquids.

Make well in middle of flour mixture and add all liquids to form a soft dough.

Knead well by hand and place in a greased warm loaf tin. (Mixture should half-fill tin.)

Leave in warm place until dough has risen to top of tin.

Bake at 425° F (Mark 6) for approximately 30 minutes.

Scotch Pancakes

20 pancakes. Each 10 C. 60 Cals. (251 J.)

240 g. self-raising flour	125 ml. water
60 g. castor sugar	butter or oil for frying
2 eggs	

> Beat eggs with water.

Sieve flour, mix in sugar, make well in middle and pour in eggs and water.

Beat until a thick batter is formed.

Heat a very little fat in heavy frying pan, drop in a dessertspoon of the mixture and cook until under side is brown. Turn and cook reverse side.

Scotch Shortbread

30 biscuits. Each 10 C. 90 Cals. (377 J.)

180 g. plain flour	180 g. butter or margarine
90 g. cornflour	90 g. castor sugar

> Rub fat into sieved flour and cornflour and work the mixture by hand to consistency of shortcrust pastry.

Roll out and cut into 30 fingers.

Bake at 350° F (Mark 3) until crisp and lightly browned. (Approximately 15 to 20 minutes.)

Shortcrust Pastry

6 servings. Each 25 C. 225 Cals. (943 J.)

180 g. self-raising flour	pinch of salt
90 g. butter, margarine or lard	water to mix

> Rub fat into flour and salt to consistency of breadcrumbs.

Mix enough chilled water to make a firm dough.

Roll out and use as required.

Shrewsbury Cakes

24 cakes. Each 10 C. 85 Cals. (356 J.)

180 g. self-raising flour	1 egg
120 g. butter or margarine	$\frac{1}{2}$ teaspoon
120 g. castor sugar	powdered ginger

> Cream together butter and sugar, then gradually beat in egg.

Add sifted flour and ginger a little at a time beating well with a wooden spoon.

Turn on to lightly-floured board, roll out very thin and cut into 24 rounds.

Bake at 300° F (Mark 1) for approximately 20 minutes.

Sultana Butter Tarts

8 tarts. Each 20 C. 175 Cals. (733 J.)

shortcrust pastry using 60 g. flour
  (or 80 g. made pastry)

60 g. sultanas	60 g. soft brown sugar
60 g. butter	1 egg (for glazing)

> Roll out pastry and cut into 8 base rounds and 8 tops.

Grease 8 patty tins and place a pastry base in each.

Mix together butter, sultanas and sugar and divide evenly between the patty tins.

Moisten edges and cover tarts with pastry tops pressing edges together.

Brush tops with beaten egg and bake at 350° F (Mark 3) for 20 minutes.

Walnut and Meringue Slices

30 slices. Each 25 C. 245 Cals. (1027 J.)

280 g. self-raising flour	140 g. ground
180 g. butter	walnuts
or margarine	90 g. apricot jam

4 eggs	60 g. grated
290 g. sugar	plain chocolate

> Rub fat into sifted flour, walnuts and half the sugar.

Separate eggs and bind mixture with beaten yolks.

Transfer to medium-sized greased Swiss roll tin and bake at 350° F (Mark 3) for 10 to 15 minutes until lightly coloured.

Remove from oven, spread with apricot jam and top with egg whites stiffly beaten with remaining sugar and grated chocolate.

Return to oven and bake until meringue is brown and set.

White Bread

Each 30 g. (weight) slice 15 C. 80 Cals. (335 J.)

720 g. plain flour	375 ml. water
5 g. sugar	30 g. yeast
15 g. lard	1 teaspoon salt

> Warm all ingredients including water which should be lukewarm.

Cream together yeast and sugar until liquid.

Put flour, salt and lard in warmed bowl and rub together.

Make well in middle and pour in yeast and warm water. Mix well together then turn on to very lightly floured board and knead well.

Return to bowl and leave in warm place until it rises to double its size.

Knead again to remove all bubbles.

Grease 1 large or 2 small bread tins and half fill with the dough. Leave until it rises to rim of tin.

Bake for 10 minutes at 425° F (Mark 6) then reduce heat to 375° F (Mark 4) and bake for a further 40 minutes until bread is brown on top and will leave tin easily.

Switch off oven, turn bread out of tin, then replace it standing upright in the tin and leave in oven for about 10 minutes.

Plain Cake

13 slices. Each 20 C. 120 Cals. (503 J.)

90 g. margarine	240 g. self-raising flour
90 g. castor sugar	3 eggs

> Cream margarine and sugar together until light and fluffy.

Beat eggs well and add a spoonful at a time beating all the time.

Sift flour and fold in.

Add enough cold water to make into a soft consistency.

Grease a 7-inch cake tin and pour the mixture into it spreading evenly with a palette knife.

Bake for 1¼ hours at 350° F (Mark 3).

Bread Rolls

10 rolls. Each 15 C. 75 Cals. (314 J.)

200 g. plain flour	¼ teaspoon sugar
10 g. margarine	1 egg
5 g. yeast	25 ml. water

> Warm all utensils, and heat water until just warm — not hot.

Cream yeast and sugar until liquid and add the warmed water.

Rub margarine into flour, make well in middle and pour in yeast mixture. Mix well together.

Remove from bowl, knead lightly on a pastry board and then return to bowl.

Cover with warm cloth and leave to rise until it doubles its size.

Remove from bowl and knead again.

Cut the dough into 10 equal pieces, put on greased baking tray and leave until these again rise to double their size.

Beat the egg and brush each role with it.

Bake rolls for 10-15 minutes at 350° F (Mark 3).

Mince Pies

10 pies. Each 20 C. 215 Cals. (910 J.)

shortcrust pastry using 240 g. flour or	
220 g. made pastry	
30 g. cooking apple	juice of 1 lemon
45 g. seedless raisins	1 egg
45 g. sultanas	25 ml. brandy
30 g. shredded suet	mixed spice

> Core apple and chop finely and mix with washed raisins and sultanas.

Add suet, lemon juice, mixed spice and brandy and mix well.

Roll out pastry and cut into 10 base rounds and 10 tops. (Make sure all the pastry is used.) Place bases on lightly greased patty tins.

Place a tenth of the mince mixture in each tin, cover with pastry tops, press edges together and brush tops with beaten egg.

Bake at 400° F (Mark 5) for 10 to 15 minutes.

Cooking with Artificial Sweeteners

Unless otherwise stated, all recipes in this Section are for 2 servings.

Desserts

Apple Crumble

Each 25 C. 265 Cals. (1110 J.)

30 g. flour	240 g. cooking apples
60 g. sorbitol	15 g. butter or margarine

> Peel and core apples, slice thinly and place in oven-proof dish with half the sorbitol.

Rub fat into sifted flour and remaining sorbitol to consistency of breadcrumbs.

Sprinkle over apples and bake at 350° F (Mark 3) for 40 to 45 minutes.

Banana Split

Each 25 C. 700 Cals. (2934 J.)

2 bananas (peeled) (120 g.)	60 g. plain diabetic chocolate
120 g. vanilla ice cream	125 ml. double cream
	30 g. shelled almonds

> Break chocolate into small pieces and melt in basin over pan of boiling water. Mix in 2 tablespoons boiling water and leave to cool.

Place almonds under grill until light brown, cool and chop roughly.

Cut bananas in half lengthwise and place in 2 individual dishes.

Divide ice cream and place half on each banana.

Pour on melted chocolate and decorate with whipped cream and chopped almonds.

Chocolate and Orange Mousse

Each Negligible C. 340 Cals. (1425 J.)

45 g. plain diabetic chocolate	15 g. butter
	15 ml. rum

25 ml. double cream	25 ml. fresh orange juice
2 eggs	grated rind of 1 orange

> Melt chocolate and butter in basin over pan of hot water.

When soft, beat well. Allow to cool but not to set.

Separate eggs and beat yolks with rum, orange juice, orange rind and cream and whisk into chocolate mixture.

Whisk egg whites until stiff and fold into mixture.

Pour into 2 individual dishes and serve chilled.

Christmas Pudding

4 servings. Each 25 C. 370 Cals. (1550 J.)

60 g. self-raising flour	60 g. fructose
60 g. shredded suet	50 ml. rum
60 g. cooking apple	1 teaspoon
45 g. stoned raisins	mixed spice
30 g. sultanas	juice and grated rind
15 g. currants	of $\frac{1}{2}$ lemon
2 eggs	grated nutmeg

> Wash and dry all fruit. Grate apple.

Rub together suet and flour. Add fructose and all other dry ingredients.

Beat eggs with lemon juice and rum and stir into mixture to form a soft dropping consistency. (If necessary add a little water.)

Pour into greased pudding basin large enough to allow pudding to rise a little, cover with greaseproof paper and steam for 2 hours.

Before serving, steam for a further hour.

Coffee Junket

Each 5 C. 80 Cals. (335 J.)

250 ml. milk	2 teaspoons
1 teaspoon	instant coffee powder
rennet	saccharin to taste

> Heat milk and coffee together until coffee is dissolved, but do not boil.

Cool to blood heat, add saccharin to taste, pour into 2 individual dishes and add half a teaspoon of rennet to each.

Leave in cool place to set.

Eve's Pudding

Each 35 C. 535 Cals. (2242 J.)

240 g. cooking apples	60 g. margarine
60 g. self-raising flour	1 egg
60 g. sorbitol	

> Cream together sorbitol and margarine until light and fluffy. Gradually beat in egg.

Fold in sifted flour. (If mixture is too stiff to form soft dropping consistency, add a little water.)

Peel, core and slice apples very thinly and place in oven-proof dish.

Spread sponge mixture on top and bake at 350° F (Mark 3) for 20 to 30 minutes.

Foamy Apple Parfait

Each 10 C. 80 Cals. (335 J.)

240 g. cooking apples   juice ½ lemon
1 egg white   saccharin to taste
30 g. diabetic raspberry jam

> Quarter and core apples and place in saucepan with a little water.

Cook until soft and pulpy, allow to cool then rub through a sieve or put through food mill.

Stir in lemon juice and saccharin to taste.

Whisk egg white stiffly and fold into mixture.

Using 2 individual dishes, place a layer of jam on base, then a little apple foam. Continue layers until all jam and apple are used finishing with apple.

Separate eggs, beat yolks and gelatine together, add cream and whisk into gooseberry purée.

Leave in cool place and when mixture starts to set, whisk again well.

Fold in stiffly beaten egg whites and transfer to ice trays.

Freeze in ice compartment of refrigerator.

Gooseberry Sorbet

Each Negligible C. 155 Cals. (649 J.)

240 g. gooseberries   50 ml. single cream
125 ml. water   5 g. gelatine
2 eggs   saccharin

> Top and tail gooseberries and cook gently in the water until very tender. Cool and rub through sieve or purée in electric blender.

Dissolve gelatine in tablespoon hot water, add saccharin to taste and leave to cool but not to set.

Lemon Milk Jelly

Each 5 C. 80 Cals. (335 J.)

250 ml. milk   10 g. gelatine
100 ml. water   saccharin to taste
juice of 1 lemon

> Heat water and dissolve gelatine. Allow to cool.

Whisk in milk, lemon juice and add saccharin to taste.

Pour into serving dish and leave in cool place to set.

Orange Jelly Whip

Each 5 C. 25 Cals. (105 J.)

100 ml. fresh orange juice   1 egg white
150 ml. water   saccharin to taste
10 g. gelatine

> Heat a little of the water and dissolve gelatine.
Add remaining water, orange juice, saccharin to taste and leave until it starts to set.
Add egg white and whisk until light and fluffy.
Leave in cool place to set.

Peach Melba

Each 20 C. 505 Cals. (2112 J.)

2 fresh peaches   125 ml. double cream
   (240 g.)   120 g. vanilla
60 g. diabetic   ice cream
   raspberry jam   saccharin to taste

> Plunge peaches in boiling water for 2 minutes then remove skin.
Cut in half and remove stones.
Poach peaches in boiling water for about 5 minutes until tender. Remove and cool.
Retain 50 ml. of the cooking water and add saccharin to taste.
Sieve jam and blend in sweetened cooking liquid.
Using 2 individual dishes, divide ice cream and peach halves, pour on sauce and decorate with whipped cream.

Peach Mousse

Each 5 C. 195 Cals. (817 J.)

120 g. fresh peaches   250 ml. water
10 g. gelatine   saccharin to taste
75 ml. double cream

> Plunge peaches in boiling water for 2 minutes, peel, cut in half and remove stones.
Slice peaches, reserving 2 slices for decoration and cook remainder in water until very tender. Rub through sieve or purée in electric blender.
Dissolve gelatine in a little of the hot cooking water, and add to sieved peaches. Leave in cool place until it starts to set.
Add cream and saccharin to taste. Whisk all together until very light and fluffy.
Transfer to individual dishes, decorate with reserved peach slices and serve chilled.

Pear Condé

Each 20 C. 340 Cals. (1433 J.)

1 pear (120 g.)   75 ml. double cream
250 ml. milk   30 g. diabetic
15 g. rice (uncooked)   apricot jam
5 g. arrowroot   saccharin to taste
   (1 teaspoon)

> Wash rice and place in saucepan with milk. Bring to boil and cook until rice is tender. Remove from heat, cool and stir in cream. Add saccharin to taste.

Peel pear and remove core, cut in half and poach in a little water until tender.

Using individual dishes, divide rice and top with pear halves.

Heat 2 tablespoons water and stir in arrowroot, cook for a few minutes until thick, blend in diabetic jam and pour over pears.

Serve chilled.

> Cut rhubarb into pieces and cook in a little water until very tender.

Make custard with custard powder and milk in usual way.

Allow to cool slightly.

Rub rhubarb through sieve or purée in electric blender, mix well with custard, add saccharin to taste and serve chilled.

Queen's Pudding

Each 20 C. 335 Cals. (1403 J.)

40 g. soft breadcrumbs
350 ml. milk
3 eggs
45 g. diabetic jam

rind and juice
of 1 lemon
saccharin liquid

> Separate eggs and beat yolks with the milk. Add breadcrumbs, lemon juice and rind and a few drops of saccharin liquid. Stand for 15 minutes.

Pour mixture into greased oven-proof dish and spread with jam.

Beat egg whites stiffly and spoon over top of pudding.

Bake at 350° F (Mark 3) until pudding is set and meringue golden brown.

Rhubarb Fool

Each 20 C. 175 Cals. (733 J.)

240 g. rhubarb (trimmed)
350 ml. milk

30 g. custard powder
saccharin

Rice Pudding

Each 20 C. 250 Cals. (1048 J.)

30 g. rice
250 ml. milk
100 ml. water

30 g. butter
saccharin

> Wash rice and place with butter, milk and water in oven-proof dish.

Bake at 350° F (Mark 3) for 1 hour.

Remove from oven and mix in saccharin to taste.

Semolina Pudding

Each 20 C. 260 Cals. (1089 J.)

30 g. semolina
300 ml. milk

30 g. butter
saccharin to taste

> Make a smooth paste with the semolina and a little of the milk.

Bring remaining milk to boil, remove from heat, add butter and gradually mix into semolina paste. Return to pan and stir over low heat until mixture thickens.

Remove from heat, cool slightly and add saccharin to taste.

Steamed Jam Sponge

Each 20 C. 520 Cals. (3016 J.)

60 g. self-raising flour	2 eggs
45 g. butter or margarine	60 g. diabetic jam
45 g. fructose	water to mix

> Cream together fat and fructose until light and fluffy. Add well-beaten eggs gradually.

Fold in flour and mix to a soft dropping consistency with water.

Grease small pudding basin, put jam in base and pour on pudding mixture.

Cover with greased paper and steam for 1 hour.

Trifle

4 servings. Each 15 C. 215 Cals. (901 J.)

45 g. self-raising flour	250 ml. diluted diabetic
45 g. sorbitol	orange squash
1 egg	50 ml. double cream
20 g. custard powder	15 g. gelatine
250 ml. milk	saccharin to taste

> Make sponge by beating together egg and sorbitol until light and fluffy, and then folding in sifted flour.

Place in lightly-greased baking tin and bake at 350° F (Mark 3) for 15 minutes. Allow to cool, and place on base of serving dish.

Dissolve gelatine in a little hot water, add orange squash and pour over sponge. Leave in cool place to set.

Make custard with milk in usual way, allow to cool, sweeten with saccharin to taste and pour over jelly.

Whip cream and decorate trifle.

Velvet Pudding

Each 25 C. 160 Cals. (670 J.)

250 ml. milk	100 ml. fresh orange juice
30 g. custard powder	saccharin

> Make custard with custard powder and milk in usual way. Remove from heat and cool slightly but do not allow to set.

Stir in orange juice, add saccharin to taste and transfer to serving dish.

Serve chilled.

Cakes

Shortbread

18 biscuits. Each 5 C. 55 Cals. (230 J.)

120 g. self-raising flour   90 g. butter
30 g. fructose   or margarine

> Cream together fat and fructose until soft.
   Mix in flour and knead well to form a stiff firm paste.
   Roll out on lightly floured board, and cut into 18 fingers.
   Prick and bake on greased baking tray at 300° F (Mark 1) until crisp and pale brown. (About 15 minutes.)

Chocolate Sponge

6 slices. Each 10 C. 180 Cals. (754 J.)

60 g. self-raising flour   60 g. margarine
60 g. sorbitol   2 eggs
15 g. granulated sugar   60 g. diabetic jam
15 g. cocoa powder

> Cream together margarine, sugar and sorbitol
   Beat eggs and gradually beat them into the mixture.
   Fold in sifted flour and cocoa.
   Grease two 6-inch sponge tins, and divide the mixture between them spreading evenly.

Bake for about 15 minutes at 400°F (Mark 5).
   When cold, spread with diabetic jam and sandwich two halves together.

Coconut Rings

20 biscuits. Each 5 C. 95 Cals. (408 J.)

150 g. self-raising flour   60 g. dessicated
60 g. sorbitol   coconut
90 g. butter   1 egg
   or margarine   pinch of salt

> Rub fat into sifted flour, sorbitol and salt to consistency of breadcrumbs.
   Rub in two-thirds of coconut.
   Beat egg well and add to mixture to form a stiff paste. (If necessary add a little water.)
   Roll out on lightly floured board and cut into 20 rings making sure all the mixture is used.
   Sprinkle with remaining coconut and bake on greased baking tray at 350° F (Mark 3) for 10 to 15 minutes.

Doughnuts without Yeast

17 doughnuts. Each 10 C. 70 Cals. (293 J.)

240 g. self-raising flour   grated rind of 1 lemon
45 g. fructose   pinch cinnamon
1 egg   pinch of salt
60 g. margarine   oil for frying

> Rub margarine into sifted flour, salt and fructose to consistency of breadcrumbs. (Reserve a little fructose for dredging.)

Mix in lemon rind and bind with beaten egg and a little water to make a stiff dropping consistency.

Form into 17 balls and fry in smoking hot oil.

Drain and toss in fructose and cinnamon.

Madeira Cake

8 slices. Each 5 C. 160 Cals. (670 J.)

120 g. self-raising flour	60 g. butter or margarine
120 g. sorbitol	2 eggs

> Cream together fat and sorbitol until light and fluffy.

Beat eggs and add gradually, beating all the time.

Sift and fold in flour.

Grease a 6-inch cake tin and bake mixture at 350° F (Mark 3) for 45 minutes.

Welsh Cakes

15 cakes. Each 10 C. 120 Cals. (503 J.)

shortcrust pastry using 120 g. flour or 160 g. made pastry	
90 g. self-raising flour	2 eggs
60 g. sorbitol	30 g. diabetic jam
60 g. margarine	grated rind of $\frac{1}{2}$ lemon

> Make pastry in usual way and roll out thinly. Cut into 15 rounds. Place each round in a greased patty tin and spread with a little diabetic jam.

Cream together margarine and sorbitol until light and fluffy.

Beat eggs and beat gradually into the mixture.

Stir in lemon rind, fold in sifted flour and mix to soft dropping consistency with water.

Divide evenly between patty cases and bake at 400° F (Mark 5) for 10 to 15 minutes.

Christmas Cake

6 slices. Each 20 C. 300 Cals. (1257 J.)

180 g. self-raising flour	25 ml. rum
60 g. butter or margarine	grated rind of 1 lemon grated rind of 1 orange
45 g. fructose	$\frac{1}{2}$ teaspoon ground ginger
3 eggs	
30 g. sultanas	$\frac{1}{2}$ teaspoon cinnamon
30 g. seedless raisins	1 teaspoon mixed spice
30 g. currants	

> Wash and dry fruit.

Cream together fat and fructose until light and creamy.

Gradually add well beaten eggs, fold in sifted flour, and mix in all other ingredients. (If mixture is too dry to form a stiff dropping consistency, add a little water.)

Line 6-inch cake tin with greaseproof paper and bake at 350° F (Mark 3) for 1 to $1\frac{1}{2}$ hours.

Preserves

Apple Jelly

Each 30 g. (weight) serving Negligible C. 70 Cals.
(293 J.)

1 kg. cooking apples	sorbitol
500 ml. water	

> Wash apples and cut into quarters. (There is no need to peel or core.)

Put in large pan with water, bring to boil and cook gently until fruit is soft and pulpy.

Transfer to jelly bag and leave to strain overnight.

Measure juice and add 480 g. sorbitol to each 500 ml. of liquid.

Return to pan, bring to boil and cook rapidly for about 10 minutes.

To test for setting, place a little on a saucer. If a skin forms it is ready to be put in clean warm jars.

Cool before covering. Store in cool place.

Apple and Blackberry Jelly

Each 30 g. (weight) serving Nil C. 70 Cals.
(293 J.)

480 g. cooking apples	480 g. fructose
240 g. blackberries	1 litre water

> Wash apples and cut into quarters. (There is no need to peel and core.) Wash blackberries.

Put fruit with water in large pan, bring to boil and simmer until fruit is soft and mushy.

Transfer fruit to jelly bag and leave to strain overnight.

Add fructose to strained liquid, bring to boil and simmer for approximately 10 to 15 minutes.

To test for setting, place a little in a saucer. If a skin forms it is ready to be put in clean warm jars.

Cool before covering. Store in cool place.

Apricot Jam

Each 30 g. (weight) serving Negligible C. 5 Cals. (21 J.)

480 g. fresh apricots   juice 1 lemon
125 ml. water   saccharin to taste
30 g. gelatine

> Wash and cut fruit into quarters and remove stones. Do not peel.

Place in saucepan with water and simmer until fruit is very tender. (About 20 minutes.) Cool slightly.

Add saccharin to taste.

Dissolve gelatine in a little of the hot cooking water and add to the jam.

Pour into clean warm jars.

Cool before covering.

Store in cool place. *Warning: this jam has a short shelf life.*

Lemon Curd

Each 30 g. (weight) serving Nil C. 90 Cals. (377 J.)

120 g. unsalted butter   250 ml. lemon juice
160 g. sorbitol   30 g. grated lemon rind
8 egg yolks

> Put butter, egg yolks, sorbitol, lemon juice and rind in top of a double saucepan.

Cook on low heat, but do not allow to boil, until mixture is thick enough to coat back of a spoon.

Pour into clean, dry, warm jars, allow to cool and cover as for jam.

Keep in refrigerator or cool place until ready to use.

Grapefruit Curd

Each 30 g. (weight) serving Nil C. 70 Cals. (293 J.)

1 large grapefruit   30 g. unsalted butter
60 g. sorbitol   1 egg

> Squeeze juice from grapefruit, strain, and beat in egg and sorbitol.

Add melted butter and transfer to clean jar.

Put jar in pan of boiling water and heat until sorbitol has dissolved and mixture thickens.

Remove from pan and allow to cool.

Cover and store in cool place. Use within 2 to 3 days.

Orange Marmalade I

Each 30 g. (weight) serving Negligible C.
70 Cals. (293 J.)

480 g. Seville oranges	juice 2 lemons
1 kg. sorbitol	1 litre water

> Wash fruit well and place, with water, in large saucepan.

Bring to boil and simmer until fruit is very tender.

Remove from pan, allow to cool then cut oranges in half.

Remove and discard pips.

Chop fruit finely, return to liquid and add sorbitol and lemon juice.

Bring to boil and cook until fruit starts to set. (About 15 to 20 minutes.) To test, place a small quantity on a saucer and, if a skin forms, the marmalade is ready to put in clean warm jars.

Cool and cover. Store in cool place.

Orange Marmalade II

Each 30 g. (weight) serving Negligible C. 5 Cals.
(21 J.)

480 g. Seville oranges	750 ml. water
juice 1 lemon	saccharin to taste
40 g. gelatine	

> Peel oranges finely leaving pith on fruit, and chop peel finely.

Remove pith and pips from fruit and chop flesh roughly.

Place chopped rind and flesh in large pan with water, bring to boil and simmer until rind is very tender.

Remove from heat, cool, add saccharin to taste, dissolve gelatine in a little hot water and stir into the marmalade.

Pour into clean warm jars.

Cool before covering. Store in cool place.

Strawberry Jam

Each 30 g. (weight) serving 2 C. 75 Cals.
(314 J.)

480 g. strawberries	30 g. gelatine
480 g. fructose	3 tablespoons water
juice 1 lemon	

> Hull strawberries, wash well and put in large pan with water.

Simmer gently until fruit is tender but not mushy.

Add fructose, bring to boil and simmer for a further 15 to 20 minutes. Remove from heat.

Dissolve gelatine in a little hot water and stir into jam.

Pour into clean warm jars.

When cold, cover jars and store in cool place.

Victoria Plum Jam

Each 30 g. (weight) serving Negligible C.
65 Cals. (272 J.)

480 g. Victoria plums	60 g. Certo
480 g. sorbitol	125 ml. water

> Wash and cut plums into quarters and
remove stones.
Bring to boil and simmer until fruit is very soft.
(About 20 minutes.)
  Remove from heat and stir in Certo.
  Pour into clean warm jars.
  When cool, cover and store in cool place.

Wines with Meals

Conal Gregory
Advisor to the B.D.A. Wine Club. Wines Controller to
Coleman's of Norwich.

The range of wines available to slimmers and diabetics is wide if care is taken over the Calorific and carbohydrate content of each wine. In general this means choosing wines that are by nature dry and that have been allowed to complete their second fermentation without the addition of sugar or a spirit which arrests fermentation and leaves an unacceptably high sugar content.

Let's start with pre-prandial wines (dinner apéritifs) and consider a number of dry Sherries. In Spain naturally dry Sherry is usually offered, but in Britain, South Africa, Australia and other countries dessert cream styles are the Sherries most often seen. The most natural dry sherry of all is *Manzanilla* — pale in colour with an attractive lemon-green hue, and a very delicate bouquet. You may detect a salty tang. This is the result of both the ageing given to the wine in the coastal town of Sanlúcar de Barrameda and in part to the soil of the district. *Manzanilla* should be drunk young and fresh and slightly chilled, if possible within three months of bottling. Such a wine is likely to retain its freshness if bottled in its country of origin. So look for the Spanish seals of origin over the neck of the bottle when ordering.

Another style of Sherry appropriate for you is *Fino.* There are basically two styles of Sherry: those that can grow a Sherry *flor* (a strain of yeast that grows like a white film on the top of the wine) and those that cannot. Those wines with *flor* have a particular flavour and quality which is to be found in a clean dry Fino. It is an unsweetened wine and has a charm of its own when drunk soon after bottling.

Like *Manzanilla, Fino* Sherry should have a delicate pale colour which, incidentally, tends to darken the longer it is in the bottle. It is made within the delimited area for Sherry production that was established in 1933, and is not taken for ageing to the coast like *Manzanilla.* This type of dry Sherry normally has carbohydrate content of up to 0.5 g. per fluid ounce and a Calorific value of about 26-30 Calories fluid ounces.

It is possible to find a Sherry that has not grown a *flor* and yet is suitable for you. This is known as a dry *Oloroso.* Rich in colour and reminiscent of the sweeter Sherries, it is in fact surprisingly dry to taste. It is known in Spain as a Palo Cortado.

The table wines of France stand out immediately as offering a number of quality wines for you. Many such wines are drunk with pleasure, traditionally with fish and poultry courses. The Loire Valley, for example, produces a number of these wines. Starting at the western estuary you will find *Muscadet,* a light dry wine made from the grape variety of the same name. The best area for this wine is the *Sèvre-et-Maine,* whilst a lesser quality wine is made from the Gros Plant grape. *Muscadet* is particularly enjoyable well chilled and served with shell-fish and other sea food. It should be drunk as young as possible and is often bottled *sur lie* which means that it is drawn directly off from the barrel without being racked and hence may have a little residual sediment.

In the region of *Anjou* and *Vouvray* in the middle of the Loire are made a number of wines which can be drunk by readers. But care should be taken to choose ones which are low in carbohydrate and Calorie value. This part of France is well worth visiting not only for its delightful wines including a few red ones like *Chinon* and *Bourgueil,* but also for the many historic châteaux which show something of the majesty and splendour that was Renaissance France. Occasionally, you may find a few Loire rosés that are sufficiently low in sugar to be drunk with enjoyment.

In the upper Loire there are two wines of particular interest — *Sancerre* and *Pouilly Blanc Fumé.* These two white wines are both made from the Sauvignon grape and this imparts a clove-like bouquet to the wine with a fruity taste. The best wines are estate bottled to retain both their crispness and authenticity. *Sancerre* is not usually as strongly flavoured as *Pouilly Blanc Fumé,* though this obviously differs from wine to wine as there are so many produced in the region. The latter is made around the village of Pouilly sur Loire, where quality dry wines are made from the Chasselas grape.

Travelling further east one encounters the white wines of Burgundy. Nowadays one has to pay a considerable amount for genuine *Chablis* (the district which lies some 100 km. north-east of the town of Dijon, a centre for gastronomic pleasure). A good *Chablis* should be both light and dry though with slightly higher alcoholic content than most of the Loire wines mentioned above. The clean fruity flavour present in *Chablis,* as well as in other white Burgundies, is primarily the result of the Pinot Chardonnay grape. Higher quality white Burgundies can age gracefully for up to eight to ten years. It is possible to drink such a wine at an older age if it is brought to life by decanting, a process that should not be restricted to red wines.

The other types of white Burgundy to look for which are suitable for readers are those from the Côte de Beaune which includes *Meursault* and the *Montrachet* parishes of *Puligny, Batard* and *Chassagne.* It is said that the finest — and the most expensive — vineyard amongst those, known as Le Montrachet, was described by Alexander Dumas as being of such high quality that "one should drink it on bended knee with one's head bowed!".

Red Burgundies make an excellent accompaniment to most red meats and particularly the dishes referred to in this book. Slimmers and diabetic drinkers should choose Burgundies that have not been excessively *chaptalised* (that is where the grower has added a sugar solution to his wine in the vat or barrel to assist the fermentation process). Although this is quite common and is usually allowed by the local wine control Appellation laws of Burgundy, a wine that has had only a small degree of chaptalisation can be taken by the diabetic or slimmer. The heavier red Burgundies from the classic areas of the Côte d'Or often fall into this category. It would be a shame to not have experienced at some stage the fine wines of this district and particularly those that offer good value for money like *Fixin, Chambolle Musigny* and villages a little further south like *Pernand-Vergellesses.* A parish wine like *Beaune* has character and is often delicious, particularly if chosen from a good or great year and possibly selected from a single vineyard although this will naturally raise the price. But be careful to limit your consumption of the heavier red Burgundies to a few on occasion.

Similar wines from the same grape varieties are grown in the United States of America. Whilst the sparkling wines from Upper New York State are certainly suitable for the diabetic, a wide range of Californian wines can also be safely taken. The Pinot Chardonnay and Riesling grapes grow well in California, particularly in the Napa Valley outside San Francisco. Certain American wines made from Alsatian vine varieties like the Traminer can also be enjoyed by you.

South of the Côte d'Or in France lie the *Beaujolais* villages though still within the Burgundy region. These wines are made with care and are often of a lower alcoholic content than their more southerly neighbours in the Rhône Valley. Small amounts of white *Beaujolais* can sometimes be found and this wine has a low carbohydrate content but only too often lacks the crispness of wines from further north like Alsace. The drier red *Beaujolais* can also be suitable and you are likely to obtain a wine lower in Calories if you select a single parish wine like *Julienas* or *Fleurie.* Readers of the novel Clochemerle will be familiar with the rolling hills and charming countryside of these parishes. Both produce attractive fruity wines.

In the Rhône Valley the grapes ripen with a higher degree of sugar because of its southerly position and the reflection of the sun from the hard soil. *Tavel,* in particular makes a dry Rosé that is probably the most suitable Rosé for

readers and can often have a carbohydrate content as low as .07 g. per fluid ounce. This wine makes an excellent accompaniment to summer picnics and is enhanced by being slightly chilled. The delicacy of the pinky hue is the result of the length of time that the freshly pressed grape juice has in contact with the skins.

Certain other Rhône wines can be found in wine shops and one of them that is often seen is *Châteauneuf-du-Pape* or its northerly cousin *Hermitage.* These wines need many years ageing before the tannin in them is broken down to give the traditional silky texture on the palate.

Similar hearty wines are made in many districts of Spain. For quality the red wines of *Rioja* are recommended. This district, named after the river Oja, a tributary of the mighty river Ebro, is famed for its quality and it can rightly claim to have introduced one of the first trade marks about 1560 when its casks were so identified. Two further factors have enabled the Rioja to produce quality wines that travel well: a suitable climate for vine production and the fact that its low vines are usually pruned to three shoots only.

Catalonia, Spain's eastern seaboard also yields a number of appropriate wines for readers, the most suitable of which is made from the Garnacha and Malvasia grapes. They produce a dry white wine of good character. Such clean-tasting dry white wines go well with fish dishes like the traditional Spanish Paella. The Conca de Barbera district of Catalonia, which lies west of Barcelona in the uplands, produces most of the drier white wines.

Portugal produces several low carbohydrate-Calorie wines of note. Probably the best known are the light wines of northern Portugal – the Minho land of the Vinho sverdes. These have an attractive charm with their fresh pétillant quality. Azal and Alvarinho grapes are grown to a height of above 7 m. or more, a system introduced in about 1920. This has had the effect of producing wines of a relatively high acidity and low alcohol (even other products of the area like melons have this acid content). Further south in the Estremadura province several white wines are made in Alcobaca, the district around the old medieval town of Obidos, whilst in the Dao region a few quality dry whites are exported.

Many sparkling wines can be appropriate for you for their low carbohydrate content. *Champagne* is unique amongst these and can vary in price from the wine merchant's non-vintage own brand through the Grande Marques to the expensive de-luxe styles which are often marketed in special bottles. The much coveted Champagne vineyards also produce a non-sparkling (still) white wine which is made from the Pinot Chardonnay grapes.

Many other districts in the world imitate *Champagne,* some by actually using the same process. Perhaps the best of these are those of the middle Loire around the town of Tours. It is said that the chalky soil in the area imparts similar characteristics in the wines. Two other districts also produce sparkling wines and the Brut (dry) quality of these make them suitable for you, as well as ordinary wine lovers. Two alternative processes are the Charmat or closed tank method which speeds the time up by making the second fermentation in a large vat rather than bottle, and the gas impregnation process, where carbonic gas is injected under pressure. Neither of these are up to the quality of Méthode Champenoise which produces the sparkling effect naturally.

A small number of *English* vineyards now yield wines that are suitable for you. Most of these are in Sussex but vineyards have also been planted in Somerset and Kent and as far north as Norfolk. The better types to look for are those made from the Riesling-Sylvaner grape varieties as the British hybrid Seyve Villard does not produce the same fruity quality.

The closest types of wines to those produced in England are the wines of Alsace and Germany. Almost all Alsatian wines are suitable for your consumption here, and each carries the name of the grape used for that particular wine rather than the district which produces the wine. The Alsace *Riesling* with its fresh grapey aroma and fruity taste and the spicier *Gewürztraminer* (particularly good with smoked salmon) are highly recommended.

The two main districts in Germany producing suitable wines for diabetic and slimming use are the *Mosel* and *Rheingau.* The *Mosel* with its charming two tributary rivers, the Saar and Ruwer, yield light, dry, acidic wines that are best drunk relatively young.

Whilst by German wine law the term *natturrein,* meaning no addition of sugar has taken place, is not allowed any longer, the quality scale of wines — known as Qualitätswe in mit Pradikat — is your assurance that the wine has been made quite naturally. Various styles are marketed which depend upon both the lateness of the harvest (and hence the ripeness of the grapes) and the alcoholic content. I would not therefore suggest drinking wine above the quality of *Spätlese* in this context as this indicates a suitable natural degree of sugar in the wine.

Whilst the *Mosel* wines have a natural tendency to be less sweet than the more commercial districts like *Rheinhessen,* I would try the Rhingau wines from further north; they have greater longevity and more fruit than most *Mosels.*

The varieties of wines available in central and eastern Europe are large but the Hungarian *Riesling* and *Sylvaner* styles are probably the most interesting (and among the lowest in price) to look for. The best district in Hungary is the Péc-Villany which lies between the Danube and Braca. The Riesling grape that grows here is of Italian origin and has a charm and flavour that is missing on the wines made in the more southerly vineyards of the Balkans.

Italy similarly has a varied range, most appropriate of which are the quality *Frascati* wines and those light, dry wines of *Soave*. They should be bottled locally to retain their crispness. Their authenticity can now be checked by looking for the initials D.O.C. on the label — the Italian Government's wine control initials.

Vines have been a natural feature of the *South African* economy almost ever since 1655 when the first Dutch settlers arrived. Today several suitable wines for readers are to be found from the vineyards around Stellenbosch and Paarl, a district west of Cape Town.

The dry white wines made from both *Riesling* and the locally-grown *Steen* vines are appropriate and it is curious to note that they are planted on American root stocks like most European vines. The white wines do tend to lack quite enough acidity to be fresh and fruity so far as the export market is concerned. A variety of fortified wines is also produced at reasonable prices, but they lack the delicacy of true *Sherry* unfortunately.

In almost every state of *Australia* wines are made, a good number of which are exported to Britain, Canada and other countries. The absence of rain in most districts — many dependent even on irrigation like South Australia's Murray Valley — means that many dessert wines are naturally made. Amongst the districts that I would particularly recommend are *Victoria* where the decomposed granite and good rainfall favour the lighter table wines and the *Hunter River Valley* of New South Wales. Many Australian wines adopt European names in their titles but increasingly regional names

and vines, like Lexia, are coming in and should be purchased for their authenticity. Several lighter red wines are made which can be excellent value, whilst the drier fortified wines are appealing, particularly as apéritifs.

The above is only a brief sketch of what to look for. Do not forget classical districts like Bordeaux for apart from the drier Clarets, there are naturally a number of white wines here that can be safely drunk by you.

Between the two rivers of Bordeaux there is the medium dry *Entre-deux-Mers,* whilst many enjoy the various styles of *Graves*. This district is, in fact, experimenting at the moment with its dry, white wines and many Châteaux which were formerly noted exclusively for their dessert wines are now partly turning to dry white wine production. This is achieved by keeping the grape juice in contact with the grape skins for as short a time as possible and often starting the fermentation process in a vat which has been injected with carbon dioxide; the effect is to find a lighter, fresher wine more along the lines of *Muscadet*.

Finally, be sure that the Calorie-carbohydrate content of the wines you choose conforms to your diet. You have a world of wines to choose from.

ALCOHOL

All drinks that contain alcohol have a high Calorie (and Joules) content, the body deriving heat and energy from the alcohol itself. This means that even when such drinks have a NIL carbohydrate value, they have a HIGH Calorie (and Joules) content and therefore should not be used by diabetics or anyone else on weight-reducing diets. Before including any alcohol in their diets, diabetics should consult their doctors.

Liqueurs are not listed as, with the exception of liqueur brandy and whisky, they have high carbohydrate values and are not suitable for diabetics or indeed for anyone wishing to lose weight.

CARBOHYDRATE VALUES

	Grams carbohydrate	Imperial measure	Metric measure
Beers and Stout			
Beer (bottled), strong and mild	10	½ pint	250 millilitres (ml.)
Beer (draught), strong and mild	10	½ pint	250 millilitres (ml.)
Stout	10	½ pint	250 millilitres (ml.)
Lager	10	½ pint	250 millilitres (ml.)
Lager, Diat Pils	2	½ pint	250 millilitres (ml.)
Ciders			
Cider, dry	10	¾ pint	375 millilitres (ml.)
Cider, sweet	10	½ pint	250 millilitres (ml.)
Cider, vintage	10	¼ pint	125 millilitres (ml.)
Cider, Bulmers No. 7	Nil		
Sherries			
All dry Sherries	Nil		
Spirits	Nil		
Brandy	Nil		
Gin	Nil		
Rum	Nil		
Vodka	Nil		
Whisky	Nil		
Wines			
Alsatian, dry	Nil		
Bordeaux (red and white), dry	Nil		
Burgundy (red and white), dry	Nil		
Chianti, dry	Nil		
Champagne, dry	Nil		
Claret, dry	Nil		
Any other dry wine	Nil		

CALORIE AND JOULES VALUES

The approximate Calorie (and Joules) contents of the drinks on this list are:

	Calories	Joules	Imperial measure	Metric measure
Beers	80	335	½ pint	250 millilitres (ml.)
Cider, dry	150	628	¾ pint	375 millilitres (ml.)
Cider, sweet	120	503	½ pint	250 millilitres (ml.)
Cider, vintage	140	587	¼ pint	125 millilitres (ml.)
Cider, Bulmers No. 7	96	402	½ pint	250 millilitres (ml.)
Stout	111	465	½ pint	250 millilitres (ml.)
Lager	80	335	½ pint	250 millilitres (ml.)
Lager, Diat Pils	117	490	½ pint	250 millilitres (ml.)
Sherry, dry	32	134	1 fl. oz.	25 millilitres (ml.)
Spirits	63	264	1 fl. oz.	25 millilitres (ml.)
Wines (red and white) dry	22	92	1 fl. oz.	25 millilitres (ml.)

Glossary

ASPIC. A clear savoury jelly used for glazing or setting moulds. Can be made with strained clear stock and gelatine, or bought in crystal form and diluted.

BAKING. Oven method of cooking.

BASTING. Spooning cooking liquids and fat over food while roasting or grilling to keep it moist.

BATTER. See Yorkshire Pudding recipe. Can be used for coating foods before deep-frying.

BEATING. Mixing ingredients together rapidly with a spoon, fork, whisk or electric beater to make mixture smooth and introduce air.

Beating meat before cooking involves hitting it with a hammer or rolling pin to flatten and tenderise it.

BINDING. Combining dry ingredients with a liquid to form a consistency stiff enough to handle.

BLANCHING. (a) Plunging in boiling water for a few minutes before peeling to loosen skins from fruit, vegetable and nuts—e.g. peaches, tomatoes and almonds. (b) Immersing meat in boiling water prior to cooking to whiten it. (c) Immersing fruit and vegetables in boiling water for a few minutes before freezing or bottling.

BLENDING. Gradually mixing ingredients together (usually with a wooden spoon) until a smooth paste is formed.

BOILING. Cooking in liquid that has reached 212° F/100° C.

BOUQUET GARNI. Mixture of fresh or dried herbs, usually contained in a muslin bag, for flavouring savoury dishes. Always remove before serving.

CLARIFYING. (a) Butter: cook in pan until bubbling ceases, cool slightly and strain through muslin or fine sieve. (b) Dripping: put in pan, cover with cold water, bring to boil and cook until fat has melted. Remove from heat and stand until fat rises and can be skimmed from surface for re-use. (c) Liquids: add lightly beaten egg white and crushed shell to liquid. Bring to boil and strain before use.

COATING. Covering all surfaces of a food prior to cooking with egg, batter, bread-crumbs or flour. (See also 'Consistency').

CONSISTENCY. The required thickness of a mixture prior to cooking. (a) Thin or pouring: batter will run easily. (b) Thick or coating: batter is thick enough to coat the back of a spoon. (c) Dropping: mixture is soft enough to drop easily from a spoon. (d) Stiff: mixture is stiff enough to stand in peaks, but too sticky to handle. (e) Soft dough: stiff enough to handle, but too moist to roll out. (f) Stiff dough: stiff enough to handle and roll out.

CREAMING. Beating fat and sugar together until appearance of thick cream, or combining yeast and sugar.

DICING. Cutting food into small even cubes.

DOTTING. Placing small pieces of fat on food before cooking.

DREDGING. Dusting all surfaces of a food lightly with flour, sugar, etc.

FOLDING IN. Introducing another ingredient into a mixture already well beaten by repeatedly passing a metal spoon to the base of the bowl and folding contents over new ingredients.

GARNISHING. Decorating a prepared dish before serving—e.g. sprinkling with chopped parsley or nuts.

GLAZING. Brushing with egg or milk before baking to ensure a brown shiny surface. (See also 'Aspic'.)

GRILLING. Cooking or browning under direct heat.

KNEADING. Working yeast or biscuit dough by hand to remove air and give a smooth even texture.

MARINADE. Mixture of oil, seasoning, herbs and vinegar or wine in which meat can be steeped for some hours to tenderise and flavour it.

POACHING. Cooking in water just below boiling point.

PURÉE. A smooth pulp obtained by putting soft foods such as vegetables and fruit through a sieve or food mill or electric blender.

REDUCING. Boiling a liquid rapidly to decrease its bulk and increase its concentration.

ROUX. A sauce base formed by combining equal quantities of melted fat and flour with a wooden spoon over gentle heat until mixture is smooth and will leave sides of pan clean. Liquid to be used should be added gradually.

RUBBING IN. Mixing fat and flour together by hand to consistency of breadcrumbs.

SEASONING. Adding condiments and/or herbs.

SHREDDING. Slicing food, for example raw vegetables, into fine strips by use of knife or coarse grater.

SIEVING. Removing lumps, skin, seeds, etc. from a soft mixture by rubbing through a metal or nylon sieve.

SIMMERING. Cooking at just below boiling point. The liquid should be just moving on the surface but not bubbling rapidly.

STEAMING. Cooking over pan of boiling water usually in a covered steamer. Fish fillets can be steamed by cooking in a little liquid such as milk on a plate, covered with another plate, over boiling water.

STOCK. Liquor obtained from the slow cooking (or cooking in a pressure cooker) of meat, fish and/or vegetables in water. Used as a basis for soups, stews, etc.

TEPID. Bloodheat—i.e. just warm to the touch.

WHIPPING/WHISKING. Beating rapidly by use of fork, whisk or electric beater to introduce air and increase volume.

Index of Recipes

Notes